DONALD W. WINNICOTT
AND THE HISTORY OF THE PRESENT

DONALD W. WINNICOTT AND THE HISTORY OF THE PRESENT
Understanding the Man and his Work

Edited by
Angela Joyce

KARNAC

First published in 2018 by
Karnac Books Ltd
118 Finchley Road
London NW3 5HT

Copyright © 2018 to Angela Joyce for the edited collection, and to the individual authors for their contributions.

The rights of the contributors to be identified as the authors of this work have been asserted in accordance with §§ 77 and 78 of the Copyright Design and Patents Act 1988.

All rights reserved. No part of this publication may be reproduced, stored in a retrieval system, or transmitted, in any form or by any means, electronic, mechanical, photocopying, recording, or otherwise, without the prior written permission of the publisher.

British Library Cataloguing in Publication Data

A C.I.P. for this book is available from the British Library

ISBN-13: 978-1-78220-559-3

Typeset by Medlar Publishing Solutions Pvt Ltd, India

Printed in Great Britain by TJ International Ltd, Padstow

www.karnacbooks.com

CONTENTS

ACKNOWLEDGEMENTS vii

ABOUT THE EDITOR AND CONTRIBUTORS ix

PREFACE xv

INTRODUCTION xvii
Angela Joyce

CHAPTER ONE
Emergence and conception of the subject (self) 1
René Roussillon

CHAPTER TWO
In between sameness and otherness: the analyst's words
   in interpsychic dialogue 17
Stefano Bolognini

CHAPTER THREE
An investigation into the technical reasons Winnicott proposes that the analyst's objective hate towards the patient has to eventually be made available for interpretation   31
Vincenzo Bonaminio and Paolo Fabozzi

CHAPTER FOUR
Meeting Winnicott   45
Juliet Hopkins

CHAPTER FIVE
There's no such thing as a baby: how relationships support development from birth to two   49
Lynne Murray

CHAPTER SIX
The irrepressible song   63
Kenneth Wright

CHAPTER SEVEN
Creativity in everyday life (or, Living in the world creatively)   77
Ken Robinson

CHAPTER EIGHT
Images and words: some contemporary perspectives on the concept of regression   91
Angela Joyce

CHAPTER NINE
The public psychoanalyst: Donald Winnicott as broadcaster   111
Brett Kahr

CHAPTER TEN
Beyond the consulting room: Winnicott the broadcaster   123
Anne Karpf

CHAPTER ELEVEN
Winnicott's paradigm shift in psychoanalytic theory and practice   133
Zeljko Loparic

INDEX   143

ACKNOWLEDGEMENTS

Grateful thanks go to the trustees of the Winnicott Trust (at the time of the conference this book grew from: Barbie Antonis, Lesley Caldwell, Steven Groarke, Angela Joyce (chair), Ruth McCall, Marianne Parsons, Judith Trowell, Elizabeth Wolf) and the representative from the British Psychoanalytic Association, Shirley Spitz, who worked tirelessly to prepare the conference during the year prior to its happening. The Trust was supported in various ways by the Association of Independent Psychoanalysts (AIP), the British Psychoanalytical Society (BPAS), and the British Psychoanalytic Association (BPA). At the BPAS we were ably assisted by Marjory Goodall without whose unflagging patience and unstinting help we could not have held the conference.

To all those who agreed to present papers and workshops and then who have given permission for them to be reproduced in this volume, we are indebted, as we are to those who agreed to chair the events. Over that weekend we were delighted that PhD students from University College London helped its smooth running by acting as stewards. The audience at the conference were enthusiastic recipients of the products of all our labours. A special thanks goes to Clive Robinson who recorded all the proceedings and photographed the participants.

Without the work that went into the preparation of *The Collected Works of D. W. Winnicott*, the conference would never have happened. General editors Lesley Caldwell and Helen Taylor Robinson, assisted by Robert Ades and Clay Pearn, completed the assembly of the twelve volumes, published by Oxford University Press in late 2016. That process was guided by the project management board, chaired by Amal Treacher Kabesh, and including Clive Morgan, Sarah Nettleton, and Emma Letley.

To our agents the Marsh Agency, Camilla Ferrier and in the past Steph Ebdon, who look after Winnicott's publications, we give our thanks. In particular, for permission to reproduce the Squiggle on p. 161 in Professor Loparic's paper.

We are grateful for permission to reproduce here the following extracts or papers:

To Oxford University Press for permission to include Vincenzo Bonaminio & Paolo Fabozzi's paper, "An investigation into the technical reasons Winnicott proposes that the analyst's objective hate towards the patient has to eventually be made available for interpretation".

To Wiley Publications for permission to reproduce Winnicott's Squiggles that were published in the *International Journal of Psychoanalysis* as part of the paper, "A clinical study of the effect of a failure of the average expectable environment on a child's mental functioning" (1965).

Juliet Hopkins's "Meeting Winnicott" was based on a chapter in her book, *The Collected Papers of Juliet Hopkins*, edited by Ann Horne and Monica Lanyado (Routledge, 2015). Thanks to Taylor & Francis for permission to publish this here.

Anne Karpf's workshop presentation was based on a longer article, "Constructing and addressing the 'ordinary devoted mother': Donald Winnicott's BBC broadcasts, 1943–62", published in *History Workshop Journal*, vol. 78, Autumn 2014, with thanks for permission to reproduce parts of it here.

ABOUT THE EDITOR AND CONTRIBUTORS

Editor

Angela Joyce is a training and supervising psychoanalyst with the British Psychoanalytical Society and a child psychoanalyst trained at the Anna Freud Centre, London. There she was a member of the pioneering Parent Infant Project for many years from 1997 and jointly led the resurgence of child psychotherapy. She now works in private practice in London. She is currently chair of the Winnicott Trust and a trustee of the Squiggle Foundation, and is an honorary senior lecturer at University College London. She has written papers and contributed to books on early development and parent-infant psychotherapy, and Winnicottian studies. Her book, edited with Lesley Caldwell, *Reading Winnicott*, was published in the New Library of Psychoanalysis Teaching Series in January 2011, and she contributed a volume introduction to *The Collected Works of D. W. Winnicott*, published in 2017.

Contributors

Stefano Bolognini is a psychiatrist and psychoanalyst, and currently president of the International Psychoanalytical Association (IPA).

He was scientific secretary and then president of the Italian Psychoanalytic Society and its representative on the IPA board for two mandates. He has published around 200 scientific papers in the most important psychoanalytic journals, and contributed to several books with specific chapters. Dr Bolognini is frequently interviewed in radio and TV programmes and in newspapers and magazines. His books are *Like Wind, Like Wave* (Other Press, New York, 2006), *The Dream 100 Years After* (as editor) (Ed. Bollati Boringhieri, Turin, 2000), *Psychoanalytic Empathy* (Free Association, 2004), *Secret Passages. The Theory and Technique of the Interpsychic Relations* (IPA New Library, Routledge, London, 2010 (translated widely), and *Zen and the Art Not to Know What to Say* (Ed. Bollati Boringhieri, Turin, 2011).

Vincenzo Bonaminio, PhD, is a training and supervising analyst of the Italian Psychoanalytic Society, and in private psychoanalytic practice (adult and child) in Rome. He is adjunct professor at La Sapienza, University of Rome and honorary visiting professor at the Psychoanalysis Unit, University College London; director of the Winnicott Institute Training Course in Child and Adolescent Psychoanalytic Psychotherapy, and of the "Winnicott Centre", Rome. He is past vice-president of the EPF and chair of the Programme Committee (2004–2008), and a member of the European editorial board of the *IJPA*. Dr Bonaminio co-edits *Richard e Piggle*, an Italian four-monthly journal of psychoanalytic study of the child and adolescent and *Psicoanalisi contemporanea*, a psychoanalytic book series. He was awarded *The Fifth International Frances Tustin Memorial Prize and Lecture* (FTMP) in Los Angeles, November 2001. His publications, mostly in Italian and English, include 130 papers and co-authored and edited books and presented papers and contributions in national and international psychoanalytic congresses.

Paolo Fabozzi, PhD, is a full member of the Societa Psicoanalitica Italiana (SPI), a component society of the International Psychoanalytical Association (IPA), and is also a child analyst. He is in private practice with adults and adolescents. He is an adjunct professor in the Department of Dynamic and Clinical Psychology, La Sapienza, University of Rome, and has been published widely.

Juliet Hopkins, PhD, is an honorary consultant child psychotherapist who has recently retired from teaching infant mental health at the Tavistock Clinic. She was a founder member in 1982 of the independent child psychotherapy training (now named IPCAPA) and this year published an edited collection of her papers, *An Independent Mind* (Routledge, 2015). In 1961 she had the privilege of being supervised by Winnicott on her work with a young child, which is the subject of her brief contribution to the conference recorded here.

Brett Kahr is senior clinical research fellow in psychotherapy and mental health at the Centre for Child Mental Health in London, and honorary visiting professor at the University of Roehampton in the Department of Media, Culture and Language. A Winnicott scholar of long standing, he is the author of *D. W. Winnicott: A Biographical Portrait*, which won the Gradiva Prize for biography in 1997, and the editor of *Forensic Psychotherapy and Psychopathology: Winnicottian Perspectives*, and of *The Legacy of Winnicott: Essays on Infant and Child Mental Health*. His latest book, *Tea with Winnicott*, has just appeared, to be followed soon by a more extended historical study, *Winnicott's* Anni Horribiles: *The Creation of "Hate in the Counter-Transference"*. He is co-editor of the "History of Psychoanalysis Series" for Karnac Books and also a trustee of the Freud Museum, London. From 2004 until 2007, he served as resident psychotherapist on BBC2 and as spokesperson for the BBC mental health campaign "Life 2 Live".

Anne Karpf is a writer, sociologist, and award-winning journalist. A columnist for *The Guardian* newspaper and regular broadcaster for BBC Radio, she is the author of four books of non-fiction, including a family memoir, *The War After: Living with the Holocaust* (Faber Finds) and *The Human Voice* (Bloomsbury). Her research on Winnicott's BBC broadcasts was funded by the Winnicott Trust. She is reader in professional writing and cultural inquiry at London Metropolitan University.

Zeljko Loparic has a PhD in philosophy and since 1984 teaches philosophy and history of psychoanalysis at different universities in Brazil and abroad. In 2005 he founded, together with Elsa Oliveira Dias, the Brazilian Society of Winnicottian Psychoanalysis (SBPW). In 2013 he founded and was elected president of the International Winnicott Association (IWA). In 2014 he started teaching the Sino-Brazilian Training Course in Winnicottian Psychoanalysis in Beijing. He authored *Heidegger Defendant* (1990), *Ethics and Finitude* (1995), *Heuristic Descartes* (1997),

Kant's Transcendental Semantics (2000), *On Responsibility* (2003), and *Heidegger* (2004), co-edited several collective volumes, and published numerous papers in national and international journals on general philosophy of science and philosophy and history of psychoanalysis (Winnicott).

Lynne Murray is Professor of Developmental Psychology at the University of Reading, and Professor Extraordinary at Stellenbosch University, South Africa. She held the Winnicott Research Fellowship in Cambridge, where the focus was to conduct research to examine the ideas Winnicott developed on the importance of the early environment for child development. This led to the setting up of the Winnicott Research Unit. Her research has focused on parent-child relationships and child development in the context of difficult circumstances, including maternal depression and anxiety disorder, and the presence of socio-economic adversity and child congenital disorder. Currently her work is focused on carer-infant/child book-sharing with Peter Cooper and other colleagues, working in Africa (Cameroon, Lesotho, South Africa). Together with Peter, she has set up a charity, the Mikhulu Trust (mikhulutrust.org), to raise funds for book-sharing in poor communities-including training in book-sharing, and the production of relevant book materials. Her book "The Social Baby" was published in 2000, and last year 'The Psychology of Babies: how relationships support development from birth to two' was published. The royalties from this book are going to The Mikhulu Trust.

Ken Robinson is a psychoanalyst in private practice in Newcastle upon Tyne, a member of the British Psychoanalytical Society, and visiting professor of psychoanalysis at Northumbria University. He is a training analyst for child and adolescent and adult psychotherapy in the North of England and lectures, teaches, and supervises in the UK and Europe. Before training as a psychoanalyst he taught English literature and the history of ideas at university and maintains an interest in the overlap between psychoanalysis, the arts, and humanities. He is currently especially interested in the nature of therapeutic action and working with regressed patients. He has provided the introduction to the first volume of the *Collected Works of D. W. Winnicott*, and has a forthcoming essay on the nature of psychoanalytic listening. He is also completing a book on basic clinical concepts in the consulting room now, rooted in Freud's, Ferenzci's, and Winnicott's theory and practice.

René Roussillon is professor of clinical and pathological psychology in the University of Lyon-II, and head of the clinical psychology department since 1989. He was awarded a PhD in clinical psychology in 1988. He has been the head of the research team focusing on "the subjectivation process in borderline and extreme situations". He is also the director of the clinical "psycho-hub" of the Rhône-Alpes region in France, a facility that he founded in 2007. In 1991, he became a full member of the Paris Psychoanalytical Society (SPP) and of the Lyon/Rhône-Alpes Psychoanalytical Group; he is a former president of that association. He has published several books in French on psychoanalysis, as well as a significant number of articles (which have been translated into many foreign languages). In 1991, he was the recipient of the prestigious Maurice Bouvet Award for his book *Paradoxes et Situations Limites de la Psychanalyse* (*Paradoxes and Borderline Situations in Psychoanalysis*). The main topics of his research work in psychoanalysis are related to psychical trauma, the analysing situation, and the various forms of transference that may prove problematic within that setting.

Kenneth Wright is a British psychoanalyst well known for his work on Winnicott. He trained with the Independent Group of the BPS and as a marital and individual psychotherapist at the Tavistock Clinic. He has lectured widely both in the UK and abroad and published extensively on creativity and the arts. His widely acclaimed book, *Vision and Separation: Between Mother and Baby* (Free Association, 1991) won the 1992 Mahler Literature Prize. His most recent book is *Mirroring and Attunement: Self-Realisation in Psychoanalysis and Art* (Routledge, 2009). He is a patron of the Squiggle Foundation and practises in Suffolk.

PREFACE

The papers in this book were given at a conference in London, UK in November 2015, to mark the forthcoming publication of *The Collected Works of D. W. Winnicott* (edited by Lesley Caldwell and Helen Taylor Robinson, and published in print and online editions in early 2017). Chapters 1–8 were plenary papers at the conference and Chapters 9–11 were three of a total of six presentations given in parallel workshops.

The Winnicott Trust was set up by Donald Winnicott's widow Clare Winnicott in 1984. Its purpose was to ensure that all Winnicott's writings should be edited and published and to advance the education of the public by promoting training and research in the field of psychoanalysis and child health. The first chair of the trust was Dr Martin James, who had been a long-time colleague of Winnicott's. He was accompanied by Dr Stella Ambache and Dr Jonathan Pedder as the first trustees. The first editors were Mrs Madeleine Davis, Mr Raymond Sheppard and Dr Christopher Bollas. Over the years, other people joined them, and the personnel changed as people retired: Dr Jennifer Johns, Mrs Helen Taylor Robinson, Ms Mary Swinney, Dr Jan Abram, Dr Sheilagh Davies, Prof Lesley Caldwell, Dr Judith Trowell, Prof Steven Groarke.

The present Winnicott Trust consists of Angela Joyce (chair), Barbie Antonis, Ruth McCall, Marianne Parsons, and Elizabeth Wolf. All are members of the British Psychoanalytical Society.

In less than twenty years after it was first established, the trust ensured the publication of as many as possible of Winnicott's hitherto unpublished writings. These were in a series of books arranged thematically: *Deprivation and Delinquency* (1984); *Home Is Where We Start From* (1986); *Holding and Interpretation: Fragment of an Analysis* (1986); *Babies and Their Mothers* (1987); *Human Nature* (1988); *Psychoanalytic Explorations* (1988); *Talking to Parents* (1993); *Thinking about Children* (1996). *The Collected Works* remained an ambition that has finally come to be a reality, and includes many previously unknown pieces by Dr Winnicott. It was published in the USA and in the UK at the beginning of 2017.

The trust has been represented by the Marsh Agency (previously the Patterson Marsh Agency) since its inception.

INTRODUCTION

Angela Joyce

The chapters in this book are based on papers given at a conference in London in November 2015, to mark the forthcoming publication of *The Collected Works of Donald W. Winnicott*. In early 2017, the Winnicott Trust brought to fruition its long-held ambition to collect together as many of the writings of Donald Woods Winnicott as could be found. *The Collected Works* (CW) (edited by Lesley Caldwell and Helen Taylor Robinson, and published in print and online editions: OUP, 2017) had been long considered since Clare Winnicott set up the Trust to manage Donald's literary estate, in 1984, shortly before her death. Many of Clare's friends and colleagues were determined that Donald's extensive and prolific writings should be edited and published. That said, the project had a chequered history since its importance was first pursued by Christopher Bollas, and then by Jan Abram, without whom, it is safe to say, the Trust would not have made the decision to undertake a *Collected Works* for at least another decade, and probably not then. The two psychoanalysts who finally saw the project through were appointed on the sudden death of Elisabeth Young Bruehl, whom the Winnicott Trust had only recently appointed as general editor following an advertising process in the *International Journal of Psychoanalysis*.

The title "the history of the present" draws on Foucault's radical reconsideration about how to think about history and the present, using a so-called genealogical rather than an archaeological model. Using this genealogical concept in relation to our thinking about Winnicott, his ideas, where they sit in psychoanalytic theory and psychoanalytical clinical development, reflects the breadth and depth of his work. Not only does it refer to his interest in the history of people, children, what happens to them in the very beginning of their lives, how that is manifested later in adulthood, but it refers to the genealogy of his ideas in the psychoanalytical movement. He sits in a particular relationship to Freud and Klein and we now think of him in terms of a very rich history of psychoanalytic thinking. The ideas of family, of richness and complexity of relationships within a genogram, is a very helpful way of thinking about Winnicott and our relationship with him.

Winnicott wrote close to two million words in his fifty-five years of productive professional life. This was writing of all forms and kinds, for both a medical and psychoanalytic readership, and for many other professional organisations, including those in education, child development, sociology, and cultural studies. Something particular about him, also, were his many talks and lectures for non-professional groups, especially for parents about them and their children, and he also broadcast much of this work on the BBC. He wrote for a very wide range of specialist journals, newspapers, and magazines, as well as sending more than 800 letters to friends and colleagues, and all this was not just within the UK, but across the world.

In *The Collected Works*, Winnicott's papers, talks, letters, occasional pieces, etc. have been organised chronologically, in the order as far as is known, that he wrote them. Helen Taylor Robinson, one of the editors of the *CW*, asked the question at the 2015 conference: what does the reader gain from a chronological collection of Winnicott's writings, as opposed to the familiar, themed book collections? She answered her own query by proposing that the reader sees Winnicott's mind at work within the process of time, on new ideas, or on topical, personal, and other ordinary human matters, as these ideas start to crystallise. The ideas come in the form of letters, obituaries, book reviews, complex professional papers, and other short notes and jottings, all of them clustered around a given place in time. The reader can trace the development of what becomes a Winnicottian approach to understanding reality, inner and outer, within the framework of the medical and psychoanalytic models.

His conviction grows as he warms to a theme—for example, the emotional life of the child, alongside his bodily ailments and symptoms. He often comes at an idea, frequently intuitively, from different angles, trying to express things to yet another, very different, audience of listeners. His forthrightness and stubborn consolidation of what matters to him on behalf of humanity is apparent, as is his capacity for jokes, his inventiveness, his religious belief, and his love for individuals and for children and their parents.

Above all, Taylor Robinson said, one can hear his voice speaking with integrity, whether one agrees with his ideas or not, as if he were talking to you directly. His writing is alive with his persona, and his persona gave itself wholeheartedly to the study of the unconscious as psychoanalysis has iterated it; and also to medical science—to health, growth, and development in the inner world, to ideas of what creativity and the imagination, as well as pathology, are, in all of us, and also to what these are in the external world of reality. He remains both a traditionalist in some ways, and also a challenging radical. You can see all this developing line of Winnicott's mind, for the first time in this chronological *Collected Works*.

In possibly Winnicott's best-known paper, "Transitional Objects and Transitional Phenomena" which appears now in the *CW* in its three versions for the first time (Vols. 3, 4, 5, & 9), he affirms the place of creativity and individuality of each of us, small or great in degree and quality—and he does so in language of his own. As we know, Winnicott posited something far-reaching here: that in our affective use of the early, concrete, yet "capable of becoming symbolic" objects and phenomena in our lives, we can, potentially, go on to become persons, that in our culture and its many manifest artefacts, can powerfully and dynamically construct reality—imaginatively, rather than accept it at second hand, or indeed contribute to its deliberate destruction. We know this happens, that human beings are immensely creative. Winnicott tries to propose how and why this might indeed come about, and thus gives psychoanalytic thinking a potency, and a force, beyond the traditional area of trying to restore greater equilibrium to the troubled psyche.

Lesley Caldwell, in her opening remarks at the 2015 conference referred to William Gillespie's obituary where he described Winnicott as "an analyst's analyst, an analyst *of* analysts (Gillespie, 1971, p. 228). He took on patients considered disastrous by others. "Colleagues would turn to him when they were in difficulties although such requests could be burdensome as he intimated to Clifford Scott in December 1956 when he wrote 'The trouble is I get analysts throwing themselves on me when they feel they will let the side down by breaking down'" (quoted in Willoughby, 2002, p. 61).

Not only did Winnicott continue to be committed to medicine and a medical approach increasingly shaped by psychoanalytic ways of thinking, he maintained, despite long-standing health problems, an intensive analytic practice of adults and children. Over many decades, he wrote letters and gave talks with a lot to say about contemporary concerns such as leucotomy, the pill, the Berlin Wall, adoption, war, feminism, the disadvantage of the rigid defended and defensive analyst, the difficulties of being with patients, maternal care, and maternal depression and its effects. He was completely incensed by the decision to nationalise the health service when it was first mooted in the early 1940s, but after 1948, he worked unstintingly in the public sector till his retirement.

He took on institutional roles, collaborated with colleagues of different schools, and was twice president of the British Psychoanalytical Society, although he was rarely asked to teach candidates because of internal politics. In their book about his influence in France, Clancier and Kalmanovitch (1987, p. 105) wrote, "Winnicott was in turn ignored, criticized, rejected, admired by his British colleagues, but in the end came to occupy what we regard as his true place, that of a subtle, perceptive clinician and original researcher."

Along with his openness, it is the breadth of Winnicott and his interests that is so striking. He was completely committed to psychoanalysis but, over and over again, he put the question of what constitutes a psychoanalytic way of working in the many situations in which an analysis is not possible. It is precisely because he was so committed to psychoanalysis, that using Winnicott offers so many different ways of thinking psychoanalytically in a wide variety of contexts.

The papers included in this volume attest to the breadth of Winnicott's interests and his continuing influence on contemporary practitioners. They range from accounts of the early developmental processes and relationships (Roussillon, Murray), the psychoanalytic setting (Bolognini, Bonaminio, Fabozzi, Joyce, Hopkins) creativity and the arts (Wright, Robinson), Winnicott in the outside world (Kahr, Karpf), to the challenge to the psychoanalytic paradigm that Winnicott's ideas constitute (Loparic).

In the first chapter René Roussillon, an eminent psychoanalyst and academic from Lyon in France, examines the question of the emergence of the "self". This is an integrating exposition of Marion Milner's concept of the "pliable medium" of the mother and Winnicott's "primary potential creativity", where the feminine and the pliable plasticity of responses are combined and articulated in the experience and sense of being of the infant. The survival of the mother is not only by not retaliating but through an alive capacity to be touched emotionally by her child. These developmental processes are not magic but emerge from psychic work, Roussillon said, the work of play. Ultimately the emergence of the self necessarily includes the emergence of the other, as another subject.

Stefano Bolognini, psychoanalyst from Bologna, Italy, and president of the International Psychoanalytical Association, contributes his appreciation of the legacy of Winnicott in the psychoanalytic setting by considering the nature of transitional space there, proposing that the intermediate area makes possible connections between the self and not-self without invasion. He considered five minimal technical tools that the analyst uses to help in the modulation of the distinction between the self and the not-self in the analytic setting. At the conference these were appreciated by the audience as they were in the realm of ordinary discourse which facilitates something extra-ordinary, including phrases that are essentially requests for clarification, and the sound "mmmm", rooted in the almost universal sound for the mother and which acts as an invitation to use the space for creative thought.

In the chapter written by Vincenzo Bonaminio and Paulo Fabozzi, two well-known psychoanalysts from Rome, they give a thoughtful account of Winnicott's famous paper, "Hate in the Countertransference" (Vol. 3, CW, 2017) based on their introduction to that volume of the *Collected Works*. In their chapter, they explore how Winnicott's paper yields an innovative theoretical and clinical picture of very early development, the place of objective hate, and the first appearance of various Winnicottian leitmotifs: the establishment of an authentic relationship with external reality; the distinction and productive exchange between reality and fantasy; the construction of the sense of being real; his search for authenticity in the feelings of analyst and patient, an emphasis that echoes through his other works of that time. They situate these innovations in Winnicott's evolving relationship with Klein and her school, articulating what they regard as his progressive detachment from Klein's influence, along with a different vision of psychoanalysis, of which he himself was probably not yet completely aware.

Juliet Hopkins, a renowned child psychotherapist, in her introduction to Lynne Murray's piece, delighted the audience with her memories of being supervised by Winnicott during her training. In her chapter, she describes her encounter with her three-year-old patient Paddy, who couldn't play. Her supervisor supported her intuitive response simply to verbalise what Paddy was doing and feeling and Winnicott spoke of the importance for children of naming their emotions, intentions, and body parts, thus rendering shared and socially acceptable what previously was only private fantasy. She evoked a liberating and facilitating supervisory environment where her own creativity was cultivated by her creative supervisor.

Lynne Murray, professor of developmental psychology at the University of Reading, had been the recipient of the first grants given by the Winnicott Trust in the 1980s and which had supported her groundbreaking research into the ongoing impact of maternal postnatal depression on the children. In this chapter, she surveys much of contemporary research and thinking about the ongoing consequences of different parental practices and emphasises the extent to which this thinking can be seen as rooted in Winnicott's original ideas.

The chapters by Wright, Robinson, and Joyce, in very different ways, explore this implicit aspect of Winnicott's work, that of shape, form, structure, both in development and in creative living. In his chapter Ken Wright (a seasoned Winnicottian psychoanalyst, fellow of the British Psychoanalytical Society) writes in the territory of Winnicott's ideas about creativity and transitional space, an area he has explored deeply in his writings. Here he is particularly interested in form in artistic creation. He draws from philosophy (Susan Langer, Merleau-Ponty), developmental research (Daniel Stern), and psychoanalysis, especially Winnicott, to draw links between the processes of creating form artistically, developmentally, and clinically.

In his chapter Ken Robinson (fellow of the British Psychoanalytical Society and visiting professor of psychoanalysis at Northumbria University) also addresses the area of culture and creativity, here contemplating creativity in our everyday lives in the world. He also draws upon the concept of transitional space to highlight the role of reality as a *frame*, within which creative engagement can take place, and the internal and environmental holding of that frame. He refers to poetry (that of William Carlos Williams and William Blake), the theatre (*Oedipus*, *King Lear*), and painting (Howard Hodgkin), as well as play in the consulting room to explore destruction within the frame in the service of creative living.

Angela Joyce, psychoanalyst and chair of the Winnicott Trust, contributes a chapter looking at contemporary perspectives on the concept of regression, particularly from the point of view of the relationship between images and words in psychoanalytic discourse. Drawing on concepts from French psychoanalysis which address the impact of early trauma, she links the concept of "regredience", elaborated by Cesar and Sara Botella (2005), to the work of Winnicott in his therapeutic consultations and the use of the squiggle game. Following Rycroft, and using DWW's model of the soma/psyche/mind, she sees the analyst's integration of this triad as the source of her imaginative elaboration of her experience of her patient, not necessarily a regressive process. She describes how in situations of early relational trauma this capacity is needed to give representational form, "figurability", where hitherto there has been none.

Two chapters consider Winnicott's legacy through his engagement with the listening public—his broadcasts by the BBC. Brett Kahr's account locates Winnicott's talents for broadcasting in his family history where his father and uncle had both been mayors of Plymouth and his mother active in public life establishing community groups for young mothers. In addition, Winnicott's own identifications with his family's Nonconformist religious background add to a richer understanding of the resources he drew on in his own nonconformity. Anne Karpf's chapter not only gives a close appraisal of Winnicott's broadcasting skills but appreciates the dynamic interplay between his spoken talks and his writing for the general public. His place in BBC history is also revealed and his role as populariser-in-chief of psychoanalytic ideas about parenting is celebrated.

The final chapter, by Zeljko Loparic (who teaches philosophy at different universities in Brazil and is president of the International Winnicott Association), is a theoretical one which propounds the view that Winnicott's contributions to psychoanalysis amount to a Kuhnian paradigm shift in the fundamental theories of psychoanalysis. This carefully researched argument is a stimulating and challenging appraisal of Winnicott's theoretical place in the psychoanalytic canon.

This book is intended to celebrate the continuing relevance and application of Winnicott's work and writings. Its contributors are among the community of international contemporary clinicians, writers, and thinkers who use this work in their own way, taking it forward and extending it in the way that Winnicott passionately insisted ideas should be treated.

Acknowledgements

Grateful acknowledgement is here given to the two general editors of *The Collected Works of Donald W. Winnicott*, who contextualised the November 2015 conference in their account of the process of compiling the *Collected Works* and which I have here drawn from.

References

Botella, C., & Botella, S. (2005). *The Work of Psychic Figurability*. London: New Library of Psychoanalysis and Routledge.
Clancier, L., & Kalmanovitch, J. (1987). *Winnicott and Paradox*. London: Tavistock.
Gillespie, W. H. (1971). Obituary. *International Journal of Psychoanalysis*, 52: 528.
Willoughby, R. (2002). *Public, Private and Secret Narratives in the Life and Work of Masud Khan*. Thesis submitted for the degree of doctor of philosophy, University of Kent at Canterbury.
Winnicott, D. W. (2017). *The Collected Works of D. W. Winnicott*. L. Caldwell & H. Taylor Robinson (Eds.). New York: Oxford University Press.

CHAPTER ONE

Emergence and conception of the subject (self)

René Roussillon

I do not think I am mistaken in thinking that D. W. Winnicott would have liked his writings and elaborations to form a possible basis for the creativity of analysts who refer to them. So I feel completely in tune with him in developing the way in which I draw on some of his intuitions to develop my own work. There are domains of clinical psychoanalysis where I still do not have the feeling that I have been able to rise to the level of his contribution; but there are others where I feel that, benefitting also from the contribution of Freud and of French psychoanalysis, I have been able to extend certain of his propositions in a way that has been useful to me in my clinical practice and in my understanding of certain pathologies of narcissism.

In this chapter I will focus on the manner of understanding D. W. Winnicott's interest in the self in connection with the place occupied by the "*Ich*" in Freud's thought; it is this "*Ich*" that I translate by "subject".

*Definition of the self, the subject (*Ich*)*

In my reading of Freud and D. W. Winnicott alike, the self, the *Ich*, or the subject comprises two interconnected dimensions.

On the one hand, the term designates the part of the psyche that is at the origin of the actions, processes, and intentions that set it in movement. It designates, therefore, the promoter of psychic life, its author, what vectorises it.

On the other hand, the term also refers to the portion of psychic life that has been appropriated by the actions, processes, and intentions of this internal author. It refers, therefore, to the portion of psychic life and of its history that the subject (self) has been able to make his own, to make "self" (*soi*). It is thus differentiated from the id which represents processes "without subject or object", processes of action expressed "in the infinitive" (Freud); it represents the part of the id that has been transformed in order to be integrated with subjectivity (self).

I think that D. W. Winnicott's contribution on the question of the subject (self) in psychic life lies essentially in an approach that questions at one and the same time its conditions of emergence and its conditions of development. I will be developing three propositions on these conditions of emergence and development.

The first concerns the conditions of subjective experience of creating/finding in which the subject can have a "sense of being" in the sense implied by the famous words of D. W. Winnicott: "First being, after doing or being done to, but first being" ("Creativity and Its Origins", 1971, pp. 84–85).

The second is related to a decisive subjective experience in the subject's apprehension of his freedom of being and of being a "subject": the experience of the conditions that make it possible for the subject to experience himself as formless.

The third determines the possibility for the subject of creating and of taking possession of the category of "subject" (self): it is known as an experience of "survival" and is at the origin of the organisation of the psychic topography, and in its later forms, of the internal organisation of the "subjective" topography, thus of the subject (self) itself.

The sense of being: creating/finding

Before representing oneself as subject ("doing or being done to"), it is necessary to begin with a sense of being ("first being"). The experience of the "sense of being" is thus the basic experience of the foundations of the subject (self).

D. W. Winnicott indicates, I think, that this experience must be sought first of all in the process of creating/finding which he describes as the foundational process of the care of a "sufficiently good mother", which calls for a slightly more lengthy commentary on the place of the object in the thought of D. W. Winnicott and of its role as a "mirror" of the subject (self) in the process of subjectivation.

One of the essential efforts of Freud was to try to free psychoanalysis and psychoanalytic theory from the doubts cast over its epistemological and therapeutic value by the accusation of "suggestion". These doubts were present from the outset, since psychoanalysis was created by differentiating itself from therapies involving suggestion, and were still there in 1937 in "Constructions in Analysis" (1937d), where doubts remain present in the accusation that psychoanalysis is based on a form of the alternative: "Heads I win, tails you lose". Indeed, Freud initially committed psychoanalysis to his theorisation of the "isolated" individual, considered solely from the point of view of his intrapsychic functioning, independently of any external influences or suggestion, and dreams appeared to him, even more than play or artistic activities, as the very model on which metapsychology should be based.

Dreams are "narcissistic" and seem to escape external influences. It was only at a relatively late stage of his work and in the wake of his text "On Narcissism: an Introduction" (1914c) that Freud would fully recognise that human psychology is also from the outset a "social psychology" (1921c). He was then sufficiently reassured as to the consistency of the psychoanalytic approach to be able, without too much apprehension, to confront the question of the influence of one subject on another. But the consideration of the fact that the object of the drive is also another subject with its own desires and tendencies, a question that was no doubt never neglected in concrete clinical practice—compare the question of seduction and more generally that of trauma and narcissistic disappointment, would never become a central theme of his theorisation. For this place to be fully recognised in the metapsychology, it would have been necessary for it to be articulated with the question (essential in his metapsychology) of hallucination. But it was only in 1937, and thus at the end of his life that he began to see that hallucination does not exclude perception and even that hallucination and perception can go hand in hand and be combined as in delirium.

Right from the beginning of D. W. Winnicott's thought—his first article concerns manic defence and the denial of reality, both internal and external—the question of the place of external reality and its links with psychic reality is present. But for him as soon as the problem has been raised, it is made more complex by the recognition of an intermediate state that mingles psychic reality and external reality, thus hallucination and perception. In this sense, D. W. Winnicott's thinking follows on directly from the final intuition of Freud in the years 1937–38 concerning the formations that are superimposed on perception and hallucination. The absolutely central process (I will come back later to this essential point) expressed by Winnicott in terms of "found/created", supposes, in fact, that the "created" breast—and how, if it is not in a hallucinatory process?—is simultaneously placed by the mother precisely where the infant creates it. The baby, the infant, can thus find outside, in perception, an object that is sufficiently similar to the one that he is capable of creating by means of hallucination. This is no doubt the first form of the "mirror" role of the first environment and particularly of the mother in the emergence of the possibility for the subject to experience himself, take possession of himself, and conceive of himself as such.

The key question, without which D. W. Winnicott's work is not conceivable, is that of the conditions required so that the adjustment of what is created by the infant, and of what he finds in the relationship to the mother, is sufficiently good for the baby to have the illusion of having created what he finds. It is also the necessary condition for the infant to be able to integrate—in his primary "omnipotence" Winnicott would say—what he finds. The intermediate formation that mixes the created object and the found object, creating a third psychic category—the category of the transitional—thereby establishes a bridge and a continuity between internal reality and external reality and avoids what appears to D. W. Winnicott to be the central danger of development, namely, dissociation.

The process of the found/created must be able to operate in both senses: the infant must find what he is capable of creating and he must be capable of creating what he finds, which presupposes a suitably appropriate environment, an environment that does not put him in a position where he cannot integrate what he finds. This is the very definition of the trauma of the defeat of creativity: being confronted with a situation that one cannot integrate, a situation "within oneself" that cannot be transformed into a situation "for oneself". The failure of the process will result in an increase in destructiveness whose intensity then appears as reactive to the traumatic character of the failure. D. W. Winnicott crossed swords in this connection with the concept of primary envy proposed by Melanie Klein. Unlike her, he believed envy and envious attacks are reactive to early traumatic situations and directly linked to the failure of the processes of integration to which they attest and thus to an inadequate maternal environment.

In D. W. Winnicott's thought the setting up of the process created/found is first made possible by virtue of the perfect adaptation—thanks to a fundamental form of primary maternal empathy ("primary maternal preoccupation")—of the mother. Then, gradually, a gap between the created and the found becomes tolerable to the extent that the young infant is capable of doing the work necessary to reduce this gap and maintain the creative illusion none the less. He will then be in a position to create what he finds, provided that what he finds is sufficiently adapted. The found/created is maintained, then, throughout the process of development thanks to the mother's initial adaptation first, and then thanks to the psychic work of the subject when he is capable of it subsequently.

Before embarking on an attempt to think through, step by step, the process underlying creative activity, I would like to make two introductory remarks to this question.

Two complementary remarks: hallucination, the malleable medium

My first remark concerns the question of hallucination in its relation with the sexual and creativity. Earlier I raised the question of the nature of the process whereby the "breast" is created; I will come back later on to the complexity of what this process involves at the level of theorisation, but I would like to point out right away that at the heart of "traditional" psychoanalytic thought this process is only intelligible if related to hallucination. That is why it is so essential to link the question of creativity up with the sexual. Hallucinatory wish-fulfilment, which I think is at work in the process of the "created" described by D. W. Winnicott, is a typical process of the drive and of drive life: the sexual and creativity go hand in hand originally, the sexual is at the basis of creativity, and creativity expresses the action of the sexual when it finds occasion to fulfil itself in the service of the ego-subject (self).

The theoretical problem stems from the fact that initially the hallucinatory process was first described by Freud—in connection with the model of dreams—as being linked to an "object-less" form of narcissism, and auto-eroticism as a process that is set up when the object is absent and in an attempt to make up for its absence. Now the hallucinatory process—this follows from Freud's late propositions and seems quite widely confirmed by the current progress in the neurosciences—takes place in all cases where there is pressure from instinctual drive tension; it is no doubt "automatic" and linked to the very functioning of the depths of the human psyche, to its impulses.

When, by means of hallucination, the process finds the object that it creates, it produces an illusion of self-satisfaction that is absolutely essential in the construction of narcissism and the process of subjectivation; the subject (self) is the one who creates and who produces the conditions of his satisfaction.

The result produced by the success of the "created/found" process corresponds to what Freud calls an illusion: the baby has the illusion of self-satisfaction, of creation; he has a "sense of being" thanks to this illusion "achieved" with the help of the mother's action. The mother thus allows the baby to transform the "automatic" hallucinatory process, in the case of an increase in instinctual drive tension, into a subjective illusion that is accompanied by pleasure, thanks to which he can partake of subjective experience. It is not yet a "conception" but a felt experience, a "subjective sensation"; however, it forms the base of the future capacity of the subject (self) to conceive of himself and to think about himself as the creator of his capacity for satisfaction.

When the hallucinated object does not find the object thus created, lived experience is at the origin of auto-eroticism provided that he has had sufficient previous experiences of creative illusion and that these have left sufficient traces to be kept "in memory" and activated in a sufficiently "realistic" manner to produce a form of comforting illusion. But, as Freud constantly pointed out, auto-eroticism remains forever unsatisfying; it is consolation.

The conception of a hallucination caused by the absence of the object is still present in many current psychoanalytic contributions in which psychic work is based on the absence or the representation of the absent object. Such a conception rests on the opposition between perceiving and hallucinating, which itself supposes that the perceptual process is a relatively passive process and not highly organised as all the contributions in the neurosciences repeatedly show. It supposes that reality is "given" and not that it is constructed as a psychic category and gradually enriched by experience. It confuses the moment when the process of symbolisation manifests itself with the moment in which it is created; it confuses the second stage of the process with the whole process.

Hallucination is the perceptual representation of the expected, desired, hoped-for object. It has to be able to lodge itself in a current perception in order to "realise" itself and fulfil itself; it must therefore find a sufficiently similar perception in the present of the subject in order to have its place there. The "sumbulon" is this first "putting together", this first union of an internal process and an external "locality". If the encounter is not timely, or not sufficiently timely, it produces a state of primary narcissistic disappointment and a sense of distress, which, if it is prolonged, is at the origin of the death-anxieties and reactive destructiveness which D. W. Winnicott regards as the central axis of the pathological processes. It is only later and once experiences of fulfilment have been sufficiently accumulated that it will make autoeroticism possible.

My second remark concerns the question of the role and place of the object in the setting-up and maintenance of the "found/created" process.

In many of his early texts, D. W. Winnicott focused above all on maternal care, "holding, handling, and object-presenting" principally, and the manner in which these different components of maternal care contributed to the healthy psychic development of the baby and of the young child. It was already possible to sense from what he said about this, that beyond maternal care proper, D. W. Winnicott was already trying to circumscribe the mother's investment and her ability to tune in with the needs of the infant's ego and thus with the emergence and construction of his subjectivity. Naturally it is during the early stages of life, through the body and sensoriality, and even sensori-motricity, that primitive communication is established, and it was to D. W. Winnicott's credit that he was sensitive to this dimension through his different studies of the primary conditions of the relationship. But it was when he put forward the mirror role of the mother's face that he made a decisive step forward in the theorisation of the general meaning of primitive communication and of its place in the emergence of the capacity of the subject (self) to take possession of himself and of what he produces.

D. W. Winnicott's hypothesis is that the function of the mother's face and of what it expresses in relation to the infant is to reflect to him his own internal states or at least messages about them. From reading D. W. Winnicott's chapter on the function of the mother's face, it is clear that while the face is undoubtedly a central element of the "mirroring" role that he ascribes to the mother, it is the mother's whole mode of presence that functions as a mirror for him. Here we have a variant of the "found/created" process: the infant must first see "himself" in the mother's face and in her bodily mode of presence, and from there he must "sense himself", but it is a variant that provides one of the keys to the process itself.

The insistence placed classically on projective processes emphasised that the infant found what he created projectively. D. W. Winnicott points out the complementary importance of the "return" processes whereby the infant internalises the reflection that he perceives of himself in the response of the primary objects to his own movements and states. D. W. Winnicott makes a fundamental contribution here to the theory of narcissism and to the theory of how the subject (self) initially takes possession of itself by describing the essential intersubjective vector involved. The infant sees himself as he is seen; he "creates" himself as he is seen, senses himself as he is sensed; reflected by the maternal environment, he identifies with what is reflected of himself.

It is necessary, I think, to make a link here with what Marion Milner has described concerning the "pliable medium". Moreover, it is no doubt rather difficult to know precisely what one owes to the other as they are so close here in the conception of the primary role of the maternal environment.

Milner emphasises the essential role in the emergence of the process of symbolisation not only of illusion but, for its organisation, of the encounter with an object that is a sufficiently pliable medium, that is, with an object capable of letting itself be transformed in accordance with the needs of the creative process of the infant. Indeed it is thanks to this sufficient plasticity that the maternal environment can fulfil its "mirror" role; it is by making itself pliable in relation to the inner impulses of the baby that it can adjust the reflection that accredits this narcissistic function.

We are now in a position to try to give a metapsychological description of the process of creativity, that is, to follow, step by step, the different moments and problems that occur in its establishment and its developments.

Metapsychological analysis of the process of creative activity

D. W. Winnicott suggests that the process originates in the hypothetical "theoretical first meal" and the first traces of satisfaction. In the light of what we know now about an infant's innate capacities, we may suppose that even before this theoretical first meal he is born with a certain preconception—to use Bion's term—of the objects and encounters that he needs for his development. A form of expectation is thus present from the outset in relation to the primary environment. But this preconception is only "potential" and its hallucinatory activation—its manner of beginning to "present" what he is expecting—must meet an object that is sufficiently close to what is expected for the process "found / created" to be established. If the experience is sufficiently satisfying, the potential will take on a first form in accordance with what it has found. A certain plasticity of the preconception must be assumed here so that it can adjust to what the mother proposes if it is sufficiently close to the baby's need, that is, if it is "good enough". We may also suppose that if, at the beginning, the adaptation of the maternal environment must be very good, as the experiences are renewed and as the baby develops, he will be able to tolerate adaptation that is not so good and do the work needed to make the match between a "good enough response" and his expectation possible. The process involves, therefore, a certain "interplay" even if it is limited, a certain "demand for psychic work" for both protagonists.

One of the particularities of this primary mode of relating is that it is "ruthless", to use Winnicott's expression; in other words, in order to function smoothly it supposes that the baby should not have to take into account the particularities of his mother's state.

There are several ways of understanding this singularity of the primary relationship. A first hypothesis is to consider that the baby is in an "object-less" state, that is to say he does not recognise the presence of an external object; he may thus be said to be "ruthless" owing to his misrecognition of the object. I am not sure that this is the right interpretation of Winnicott's position, for it does not tally with the term "ruthless". I would prefer to consider that the need of the baby is to meet a pliable medium or environment that adapts to his needs, that he is born with such a preconception, that of an object capable of effacing (of "sacrificing") its desires and its own states, and that, in a certain way, this is a particularity of the first "breast" for him, a particularity of the creativity reverberated by the first breast. An encounter rather with an object that "wants" to be used ruthlessly and that adjusts itself to the baby's needs. This is doubtless not unrelated to what Winnicott calls the "pure feminine" and which may perhaps be thought of as a characteristic that is common to the feminine and to the "maternal".

I referred earlier to Marion Milner's idea of the "pliable medium", the idea of an object that is capable of assuming all forms because it has none. A link can also no doubt be made here with Daniel Stern's "regulatory self-object" and Christopher Bollas's "transformational object".

My feeling is that the "logic" of D. W. Winnicott's thought finds its indispensable complement in the idea that the first breast must be "pliable". Conversely, the primary identification, that which underlies the sense of being and which Freud identifies around the form "I am the breast", establishes for the baby a space of creativity based on the introjection of this characteristic of the encounter with the first object, with the "pure feminine" of the object, its pure feminine or its "pure maternal dimension". Primary potential creativity, the feminine, the pliable plasticity of responses are thus combined and articulated in the experience and sense of being.

Formlessness and creativity

I have just proposed a bridge between diverse propositions of D. W. Winnicott; it seems to me that this is justified by the conception that he puts forward of the importance of experiencing moments of "formlessness" in the primary relationship with the maternal caring environment. This experience also seems to me to be essential in the capacity of the subject to have a sense of his own being ("first being").

The experience of the breast as found/created is not the only aspect of the emergence of creativity; it is its quasi-biologically programmed point of departure, if my hypothesis is accepted of an innate preconception of the adjusted breast, adjusting itself to the baby's expectations. Real creativity supposes that this first experience is appropriated by the subject (self), that he makes something of it that is no longer a quasi-automatic experience but an experience under his control, a freely appropriated experience.

In 1920, Freud pointed out that the first urgency of the psyche is to be able to control what it experiences; it must "tame" its experience, to use the metaphor Freud generally employs. He also emphasises that the subject (self) must "present" the experience thus tamed to himself in order to be able to really appropriate it. In France, Green has laid great stress on the fact that "time when it occurs" is not "the time when it acquires significance".

D. W. Winnicott complements and makes an essential contribution to the metapsychology of the integrative process of working over subjective experience by underlining the necessity with which the infant is faced of experiencing formless states. These represent moments during which the baby, without being subject to any external or internal constraints—he is neither hungry nor tired, nor is he in danger from an internal need or under pressure from an external exigency coming from the environment—can let himself be and allow the return of traces of earlier experiences that need to be integrated. The formless states in question are not so much states in which form is lost, disorganised states, states of chaos, etc., but rather states of receptivity to what presents itself, of what makes its return during this state of inner letting-go; they suppose a "containing" and "sustaining" maternal environment. This formless state is the "pliable medium" part of the baby's subjectivity.

If the first phase noted by Freud is one of "taming" experience and the drive impulses that have cathected it, this phase of "control" over experience is simply a preliminary to the process of appropriation; it is only the condition for it. The subject (self), relaxing his control over the lived experience, must still "present" again to himself what he was previously confronted with in order to "give" it to himself and to appropriate it more fully. This second phase is one of putting experience back into play again, of the emergence of symbolisation through the processes of reflexive returns that it operates. But this phase is only possible if the baby has a space of welcome, a space of receptivity for earlier experience, for all the earlier experiences, that is to say a space that is sufficiently formless to welcome all of them potentially.

This "formless" space results from the apperception of the plastic capacities for adaptation of the maternal environment, from the meeting between the baby's need to find an environment capable of adapting specifically to his needs and impulses and a sufficiently "plastic" and "pliable" environment. This indeed is why, at the beginning, the adaptation of the maternal environment must be almost perfect; it is vital that the baby also has the experience of an environment that is not "perfect" from the outset, but which shows signs of a certain "tension" and effort towards adaptation and adjustment. The experience of the effort of adaptation of the maternal environment is just as important, if not more so, than the result itself, and in any case more than an adaptation that is immediately "magically tuned" to the baby. It is important for forging the experience that a transformation is possible, that it is possible to gradually create an adapted environment. It is thus decisive for the founding of hope; as D. W. Winnicott points out on various occasions, a "magic" environment doesn't have much value after a certain degree of development. There is no contradiction between what he proposes and the notion, so important for Freud, of "psychic work"; it is simply that for Winnicott, "psychic work" is a "work of play".

But, once again, this work supposes an adjusted/adjusting environment; it again supposes a maternal empathy with the evolution of the psychic need of the infant.

Survival of the object and the dialectic creativity/destructivity

I have just evoked the question of the "survival" of the object; it governs the vast question of the relations between creativity and destructivity in Winnicott's work in the emergence of the subject (self), and any theory of creativity must be articulated with a conception of the place of destructivity. For Winnicott this latter question is at the centre of the process of disillusionment, which is itself at the heart of the recognition of dependence and love alike.

From the moment the object is created/found, the infant has an experience of primary illusion which has its place at the heart of the narcissism of origins; he has the illusion that the object that he has in fact "found" outside is the fruit of his own inner creation. The illusion is fruitful insofar as the illusion of creation contributes to the construction of a core of self-confidence that is superimposed on trust in life and the world, but it rests on an illusion that must gradually be left behind without the capacity for illusion being destroyed. For Winnicott this process involves a particular experience for which, by analogy with the experience of the "created/found", I have proposed the name of the "destroyed/found", or alternatively of the "destroyed/lost/found".

As I have already stated, the perfect adaptation of the maternal environment at the beginning of life does not last and this adaptation, though it must remain globally "good enough", will gradually have to make way for a more approximate adjustment which is necessarily and inevitably characterised by failures.

When these occur, the infant has an experience of failure which undermines his capacity for creative illusion; he has the impression that he has destroyed it which makes him experience a form of despair mixed with impotent rage: an experience of destructivity. The evolution of this experience depends on the "response" of the maternal environment to the destructive rage expressed by the infant. This is where the concept of the "survival of the object" proposed by Winnicott in his (1968) paper, "The Use of an Object" acquires its full meaning. The object must "survive" the expression of destructiveness, that is, Winnicott adds, not resort to "reprisals" either in the form of active retaliation or in the form of emotional withdrawal. I would add a characteristic that, I think, is implicit in Winnicott's thought, for he only evokes negative properties, and this is that the object must show that it is alive, that is, creative. Surviving does not mean not being touched or affected by what the baby communicates of his distress and his impotent rage; surviving means maintaining or re-establishing the link that existed before.

If the object "survives", then the infant has the experience that what he thought he had destroyed has in fact not been destroyed; he then discovers that the object eludes his omnipotence, that the object resists this, and the infant discovers that the object is another subject (another self), whose mode of presence, whose inner desires and impulses are not dependent on him, even if they are connected with him. If the object has functioned as a "mirror" of the baby's inner states, it can also partly escape this relation "as a double" and be different.

This is the moment to make a few remarks on the "discovery of the object". All the current studies relating to early childhood are agreed on considering that the infant perceives very early on the separate existence of his mother and the people of his primary environment; strictly speaking there is no "pre-object stage" as it was once suggested. The problem is not one of "perception" but one of "conception"; it is one thing to perceive the object as being separate, but quite another to conceive of it as "another subject", that is, as possessing its own desires and impulses. What is at stake in the object's experience of survival is not, cannot be, for it would have no meaning, one that concerns the perception of the object; rather, it is a matter of conception. The experience makes it possible to discover that the object is outside, but outside the subject, which I propose, in order to underline this aspect, to name another subject (*un autre-sujet*). To put things more clearly, since both go together and are produced in the same movement, to conceive of the object as "another subject" is also to conceive of the question of the subject, and thus to conceive of oneself as subject. Subject (self) and another subject (another self) are discovered no doubt in one and the same movement; it is the category "subject of ", which neuroscientists call "the agent", which is thus the result of experience.

Winnicott gives in this connection a fundamental indication when he stresses that after going through the experience of being the "object who survives" the infant's destructive rage, the latter is then capable of a series of new subjective operations. He can differentiate, Winnicott notes, between the fact of destroying the object in fantasy and real destruction and thus grasp the fact that he can be the subject of an inner movement that is differentiated from its external effect. It is therefore conceptual categories that can thus begin to be built up and which can give meaning to perceptions, sensoriality, and even instinctual drive functioning.

Another important consequence, noted by Winnicott, is the emergence of love proper. The sequence that he describes is worth citing fully:

> "Hello object! I destroyed you. I love you. You have value for me because of your survival of my destruction of you. While I am loving you I am all the time destroying you in (unconscious) fantasy. Here fantasy begins for the individual." (1971, p. 90)

As one can see, it is the whole topographical organisation of the subject (self) that depends on going through sufficiently well the experience of the destroyed/lost/(re)found.

References

Freud, S. (1914c). On narcissism: an introduction. *S. E., 14*: 69–102. London: Hogarth.
Freud, S. (1920g). *Beyond the Pleasure Principle. S. E., 18*: 1–64. London: Hogarth.
Freud, S. (1921c). *Group Psychology and the Analysis of the Ego. S. E., 18*: 65–143. London: Hogarth.
Freud, S. (1937d). Constructions in analysis. *S. E., 23*: 255–269. London: Hogarth.
Green, A. (2002). *Time in Psychoanalysis*. London: Free Association.
Winnicott, D. W. (1968). "The use of an object" and relating through identifications. In: *Playing and Reality*. London: Tavistock, 1971.
Winnicott, D. W. (1971). Creativity and its origins. In: *Playing and Reality*. London: Tavistock.

CHAPTER TWO

In between sameness and otherness: the analyst's words in interpsychic dialogue

Stefano Bolognini

Some authors have the power to change something deeply in our lives. This happened to me particularly when I read *Playing and Reality*; my admiration, my debt, and my huge gratitude to Winnicott will be evident in this chapter. I will describe some specific passages that can occur between patient and analyst when an interpsychic activity is working.

As a specialist of the theory of technique, my main interest here is the meaning and the consequences of possible Self/Not-Self modulation in the individual mind and in the analytic pair, and its monitoring by the analyst in analytic work.

I will first differentiate the interpsychic from the transpsychic exchange; then, I will present my personal vision about the difference between interpsychic, intersubjective, and interpersonal, and its consequences for the analyst's words and style in the session. Finally, I will explore some specific technical tools, relating to the modulation of distance and differentiation inside the analytic pair.

Interpsychic, intersubjective, interpersonal

The interpsychic exchange (Bolognini, 2008, 2014a) is a natural and shareable process of mutual understanding and interaction between two human beings.

Its bodily equivalents are the physiological ways of concrete interchange between the insides of two people, equivalents of a good "breastfeeding/sucking" between mother and baby, or of a good interpenetration between adults in sexual intercourse. Both imply the passage of internal contents from one person to the other, in a situation of intimacy.

As we know, it is not only material elements (like milk, or sperm, or tears) that can be conveyed from one "into" the other, but also words, ideas, and emotions, the psychic equivalents of those elements.

A good interpretation is something like that.

On the other hand, the transpsychic relationship (Kaës, 1993; Kaës, Faimberg, Enriquez, & Baranes, 1993; Losso, 2000, 2003) is characterised by intrusion, violation of the boundaries against the other's wishes, an unbearable and unelaborable experience where the other's body and psychic apparatus is flooded with negative and sometimes destructive affects.

I want to further differentiate the interpsychic from the intersubjective and the interpersonal, concepts that may overlap or be interchangeable, but more frequently are not.

"Being a subject" does not always amount to "being a person", and *vice versa*: one condition doesn't exclude the other, but it doesn't necessarily include it either.

A "subject" could be described as a human being, able to experience his (or her of course) emotions with a good sense of self-continuity and with a cohesive perception of Self, even if the separation process is not completed and the personal boundaries are still not being defined. By experience, I could say some artists could well represent this functional level.

A "person" is a human being with a well-defined identity, with clear bodily and psychic boundaries in self-representation, and distinction from the other, even if the contact with his own Self can be relatively poor. A relevant part of his mental activity can be developed at a conscious level, with all the issues and defences that psychoanalysis has explored. A person can be defined as such even if having a tenuous contact with his subjectivity. I could say some engineers seem to typically function this way.

The interpsychic is an occasional way of co-experiencing and co-working that connects two individuals (close to Widlöcher's description of this mental collaboration, 2003), rather than a structural and stable condition.

When a mother breastfeeds a baby, there is no declared personal "status" but there can be a natural cooperation between mouth and nipple that allows both mother and baby to "work together" (Segal, 1994), in a regime of cooperation.

The two exchange both bodily and emotional contents, through specific organs covered by the membranes (mucosa) that facilitate the passage of those contents from outside to inside, and *vice versa* (Bolognini, 2008).

As analysts, we take into account that these bodily relations, initially experienced with a low level of mentalization but a high level of imprinting, will work as intrapsychic equivalents mainly at a preconscious level (as often will happen later, in the creative processes). They may become conscious and find a full mental representation, but equally they may not.

And we know that the way the preconscious is connected or not connected with the conscious is a fundamental, characteristic element of each individual intrapsychic life, on one hand, and of each individual interpsychic attitude on the other (Bollas, 1987; Green, 2000).

Among the many concepts related to interpsychic functioning, I especially mention the transitional area, which makes intersubjective cohabitation possible. Thanks to its protective action the Self is not traumatically invaded by the Not-Self; it allows the individual to experience sustainable interactions between two psychic apparatuses, without an experience of violation.

Another important point is that in the interpsychic exchange there is no confusion: a pre-subjective and co-subjective area of sensations, feelings, and thoughts can be shared, while maintaining at the same time and at other levels, individual ways of psychic functioning, characterised by a condition of good-enough separateness (Guss Teicholz, 1999).

An anecdote: on the buses in Bologna

One woman leans forward to another in front of her and comments on some minor thing that might have caught both their interests (it might have been the young lad who brusquely pushed his way off the bus; or the delighted face of the little girl holding her grandfather's hand on her adventure into town; or something similar).

The other replies in a friendly way, tuning in to the same wavelength; and so begins a little impromptu dialogue, based on commenting out loud.

Please, note, this is not the blind, disturbed (and often disturbing) speech of the psychotic who does not recognise otherness: here the otherness is clearly recognised, and with it the possibility of an exchange in an intermediate space. It is taken for granted as implicitly accepted and acceptable, provided the exchange is shareable and not intrusive for the other person.

My fantasy is that Winnicott would have been most amused to observe these little "sketches" in Bologna.

And Bologna also has at its disposal an architectural intermediate space—its 40 km of porticoes—which are neither home nor street and which lend themselves to conversation, by virtue of being neither "inside" nor "outside" in any absolute sense.

Let's go back to the bus, which is another potential Winnicottian space, under certain circumstances.

The object proposed in that intermediate space by the first woman attracts the second who "makes herself at home" on the same mental and relational wavelength and responds in her own way in an interpsychic environment that plays out in a sort of non-confusive extension of the Self.

And so begins an "on-the-bus" conversation which is not a personal dialogue, as neither introduces herself or offers any details about her own life; the aim is to declare thoughts and feelings that can be shared with each other, taking care not to go beyond the bounds of that intermediate space in which the Self and the Not-Self can meet.

Through exchanges like this the world becomes an easier place to live in and share; the conversation lasts for a few stops and when one woman gets off the bus they will politely bid farewell to each other, probably without even remembering what the other looks like.

They will not greet one another if they ever meet again because these two people do not know each other.

They simply shared a limited interpsychic area, for a few bus stops.

This was mainly an interpsychic exchange, not an interpersonal relationship.

Reflections in the clinic

For an intersubjectivist, the interpsychic may constitute a category that is relatively unfamiliar, and initially difficult to understand because it concerns phenomena of coalescence, exchange, and possible cooperation between areas and functions of two minds, which do not necessarily correspond to two subjects in any strict sense.

There is a basic functional physiology, in the relationship between two mental apparatuses, without the involvement of more structured levels of subjectivity.

I have also witnessed occasional interpsychic exchanges with schizophrenics where the cohesion of the patient's Self was scarce and the subjectivity was not gathered together at all: it was an interpsychic exchange, not an intersubjective one; nor was there any interaction as people, "in a highly personal way" (Greenberg, 2001).

Yet "the mouth opened for eating and something could go in": for some moments, the two interlocutors thought and "worked" together.

Some proposals, different functional/relational levels

For example, with a person to whom I feel it is appropriate to propose an increase in the frequency of sessions,

"So, Mr. Bianchi: here we are. Do we want to add a fourth session, after we have worked extensively at three sessions a week?"

(This is a dialogue in a primarily conscious functional interpersonal regime, between the central ego of the analyst and the central ego of the patient.)

With a subject, however, I might say:

"If we added a fourth session, do you feel that this could help you?"

I appeal, in this case, to the subjective experience ("do you feel?"), without trotting out "Mr. Bianchi", that is without formally addressing the person; instead I concentrate on the subjective and intersubjective experience that we could share and discover. The emphasis is more on the experience of the Self and less on the borders of identity.

In an interpsychic situation, I might say:

"After your comments about feeling hungry, I'm wondering what it might be like to have four sessions a week; has something similar crossed your mind?"

In this way, I would call the patient to an associative cooperation between us and a shared contact with the experience of the Self; if you like, this is another way of sharing the "porticoes", the "membranes/mucosae" and of putting them to work jointly, analytically speaking.

The interpsychic dimension is potentially universal and ubiquitous, but it does not imply that in that moment a functional level of self-representation is at work, appropriate to separate subjects who recognise the other as such (even if it is clear the subject should have reached such a level at least partially, as an advanced point of his general psychic development).

In this sense, Judith Guss Teicholz (1999) noted how mother–child or analyst–patient interactions entail constant reciprocal regulation, but not necessarily constant, explicit reciprocal recognition: this official conscious acknowledgement may sometimes be technically "useful", but not always.

The interpsychic may concern pre-subjective (as well as co-subjective) shifting levels of functioning, it can be occasional or discontinuous, but the patient usually maintains a central position in the mind of the analyst.

The interpsychic is a level of "broad band" functioning, in that it allows the coexistence of mental states in which the object is recognised in its separateness, alongside other mental states where this may not be so clear. This is a temporary and transitory condition of companionable and cooperative "fusionality" (Bolognini, 1997a, 1997b, 2002; Fonda, 2000), part of the normal, mental cohabiting of human beings.

In those moments the overt recognition of separateness is not necessary.

The image of the "cat flap", which I used in my book *Secret Passages*, comes in handy as a symbol of something different, intermediate between the opening of the complete "interpersonal" door (behind which you find the person) and a clandestine breaking-in of the "transpsychic" cracks exploited by the mice, where the cat is unable to pass.

The cat flap device corresponds topically to a preconscious mental level, and relationally to an interpsychic level, which does not imply the "official" (= interpersonal) opening of the door, but equally does not correspond to the unconscious cracks and "transpsychic" transmission levels on which the "mice"/pathological projective identifications carry out their actions.

Analysis "constructs a cat flap", and "trains the cat" to use it (the cat being a preconscious portion of the ego that is quick at intuitions and associations). In the interpsychic exchange, we often accept implicitly—but also instinctively, consensually, and with a significant saving of energy—that "the cat" comes and goes, back and forth between ourselves and others.

At times we see and notice it, unclear here what the cat is, at others we do not; its passing is a natural, non-invasive, and non-parasitic event that is not subject to rigid control and that generally does not disturb us. This is probably a crucial part of our "knowing how to get by in this world" and more important than we are normally led to believe.

Finally, I think the interpsychic occurs relatively rarely, when an analyst is particularly well tuned to himself, and then to the patient's internal world and dynamic organisation; this enables the transmission of combined verbal/sensory elements from within the analyst to within the patient, in an unforced way and in a regime of "informed consent" where, through the collaboration with the conscious central ego, the patient gradually becomes aware of the transformations in progress.

Five minimal technical tools

All analysts use a variety of minimal tools in their everyday practice, and they do so, more often than not, in a natural, almost instinctive way: these technical tools pass through the "cat flap", not because they are unconscious, but because they are essentially and consensually experienced as ordinary.

In them, the modulation of the distinction between Self and Not-Self plays a key role.

Although rarely found in analytic literature, these tools deserve to be mentioned and described, since they are less banal and less obvious than they might appear.

First tool

The first regards phrases that are essentially requests for clarification, "conversational" questions we sometimes ask patients during their associative flow or non-flow, when we feel that something is really missing, or not being said, and so on. I will mention three:

1) "That is …?", when the patient has said something that is not clear to us.

2) "Such as …?" This is a more mischievous question, a kind of "extractor of further thoughts" I might use in an attempt to get patients to work on the descriptive and qualitative aspects of what they are saying, so that they go further, say more, and get into the emotional colour, temperature, and quality of potential similarities with other situations.
3) "How so …?" This question is even more sneaky, intriguing, and potentially demanding.

All these technical tools of the analytical situation seem destined to stimulate the patient's central ego. The patient is spurred on to complete a secondary process that was touched on but interrupted, and aims to clarify the meaning of reticent, elusive, allusive, incomplete, or otherwise incomprehensible communications.

Deep reflections on these technical aspects have been presented by some authors, like F. Busch (2014).

Anyway, the relational aspect evoked by these brief expressions (*"That is?"*, *"Such as?"*, *"How so?"* …) is potentially very complex.

First the object (the analyst) expresses an interest in the thoughts and the feelings of the other. He (or she of course) does not go along with the implicit regime of incomprehension that the subject (the patient) tends to set up for the analyst, as others had once done to him. The analyst shows he has understood that the patient's defensive ego is opposing the process of understanding and communication, and does not passively accept the censorship and functional castration that constitutes this resistance.

These kinds of question ("That is?" … "Such as?") openly reveal the lack of omnipotence of the analyst by declaring his inability to understand or know without the patient's help, and they come from a relational level of partial symmetry and of unsettling, yet useful, similarity between them.

If they are not presented in a superego-ish way, they appear to come "from the same height" and not from above; the modulation of "sameness" and "otherness" is crucial to their effectiveness.

They also provide the patient with a direct experience of the analyst's capacity to accept his own limits and the castration of his own illusions of omnipotence (so different from the implicit "I know everything, I understand everything"). This means he can go deeper into the real situation and the relationship in the analysis.

Asking, in these cases, is an exercise of humility and realism; knowing how to ask offers the patient a contact with the acceptability of not knowing, without this meaning a narcissistic defeat. In many cases offering a partial symmetry such as: "Help me understand …", or "Imagine, this situation …" greatly facilitates the patient's willingness to collaborate.

The analyst shows an underlying calmness and security, and the patient can experience the analyst's natural and relaxed manner, condensed into a split second, in dealing respectfully with his own "ego that has not understood". Overcoming the shame of his own limits can be facilitated through the direct experience of seeing how the analyst deals with his "not knowing".

I should specify that this is not a corrective experience *tout court*, but rather an experience of how the other deals with his own Self.

However, an excessive display of naturalness by the analyst can also produce the opposite effect, as it can humiliate the patient and make him envious of such a capacity.

The third question: "How so …?" or "In what way …?" has a rather different specificity in that it does not suggest the patient is being reticent, unlike "That is …?" and "Such as …?" It asks for something more, a progressively deeper study with a view to potentially interesting outcomes.

The analyst, in this case, is openly investigative and yet does not pay a particular narcissistic price. Asking "How so …?" or "In what way …?" is not only about a possible lack of knowledge or understanding, it is because he is interested in something more, in a further exploration; therefore, narcissistically the analyst is less diminished by the fact of asking.

In all these cases, the patient is being asked to work harder, not to stop on the threshold of the unsaid or the incompletely said. The analyst could be compared to a coach who engages the pupil intensively, stimulating him to do a better representational and communicative job. The step from being facilitating to being intrusive and persecutory can be a short one, so the analyst needs to be able to ask for an extra effort without taking the patient to breaking point.

A possible consequence of asking may be the premature or too abrupt deflation of the idealisation of the analyst since if the analyst ("subject/object—supposed to know" …) asks, it means that he does not know, and this may be prematurely disappointing, if the timing for de-idealisation in the course of the analytic process is not right.

As usual, the analyst must monitor the defensiveness of the patient's mental apparatus; the analytic exchange is made up of subtle perceptions and modulations of "how much reality can be tolerated" (Micati, 1993).

Second tool

I now turn to my second minimal technical tool, the use of the universalising, impersonal pronoun instead of a personal pronoun or name (in English with the impersonal pronoun "one" in more formal language, or "you" in more informal situations, to refer to "people" in general).

Curiously, it is to Irwin Yalom and his historical textbook on group analysis (1970) that I owe my interest in this, in what he called the "universality of experience". After all, even if the group dimension can evoke a potentially greater sharing of experiences, the pair relationship in analysis is equally affected by this process, which significantly reduces the gap between "sameness" and "otherness".

The use of the impersonal pronoun is the extension of the patient's experience to all human beings, to their common condition, and it limits any apparent abnormality and at times can even reshape pathological characterisations.

Many patients fear that what they are experiencing is in itself evidence of a severe and untreatable pathology so when we use the impersonal pronoun "one" or "you" (just as when we use the collective "we") it has the effect of diluting, extending, and further humanising the difference between Self and Not-Self, and reducing anxieties about confrontation, judgement, inferiority, indignity, and unacceptability.

The idea that, under certain circumstances, the internal effects experienced by the patient can be linked to understandable processes of life can make it possible to examine them in a more thoughtful and analytical way. The quality of the experience can be explored in a deeper way and the control by the defensive ego is made less obsessive.

We use the impersonal pronoun in the session when it is useful to modulate this universality of experience.

Third tool

The third analytic technique is the sound, "Mmmmh …"

In 1954, Ralph Greenson devoted a short but intense theoretical-clinical paper to the expression, "Mmmmh …!", noting how it corresponds to oral pleasure and how it is connected to the "m" the root of "mother, mamma, mére" etc.

Greenson dwelt above all on the pleasure aspect, but I would like to emphasise the experience of a shared co-thinking contact not far removed from Greenson's reference to the pleasure of sucking, in a state of "non-confusive fusionality", in which the distinction between the Self and the Other becomes blurred.

The "Mmmmh …!" sound is an implicit invitation to share a level of reflectiveness, favoured by a pause: it gives the feeling of a mind at work, the creation of a space available for thoughts.

It is certainly a very different dimension from what I have called the "empty void" created by a "hard" silence on the part of the analyst (Bolognini, 2014b), that aims at "flushing out" the patient's unconscious by destabilising the defensive ego.

There are situations where "hard" silence permits the perception and the dramatisation of a useful void, open to the exploration of what is new, and where it has a powerful function of "sucking out" the internal contents. But there are others where the analyst's silence may distance the Self too much from the Not-Self: it can freeze or block the patient, and can also send him into a panic.

The "Mmmmh …!" sound on the other hand bears witness to the analyst's interest, it creates an available space for the patient, and encourages a possibility of shared thought that may be activated as a model, such as: "… do as I do! Try and feel these things. What do they bring to mind for you?"

"Mmmmh …!" is basically an invitation to work together reflectively.

Fourth tool

Another technique is the simple repetition of what the patient has said, with the inevitable addition of the analyst's preconscious resonant nuances.

Here is a brief clinical example:

The patient had started the session commenting on the news: an Alitalia Airbus had landed at Fiumicino airport without its landing gear. Then, it brought a dream.

P: In the dream, I was inside a vehicle, perhaps a van, flying, gliding downwards. I was in the passenger seat. It was clear that we were going to end up in an expanse of muddy, murky, brown water.

A: Ah! ... The van ... (pause) ... glides ... (pause) ... towards an expanse of brown water ... (pause) ... full of mud ... (pause) ... and you are next to the driver ... (pause) ... who cannot be seen, though ... (leaves it hanging) ....

P: (laughing) Sure, hearing it repeated like that ... you can't help but think that it was me next to you! ...

A: In short, it's about landing without getting hurt ... even if it involves making contact with water that is not exactly crystal clear ...! [The patient must "come down" from an idealising position to one that is more realistic, about himself and the object.]

Fifth tool

My final example of a minimal technical tool is: the targeted and intentional use of "we" in specific communicative passages, aimed at producing functional synergies and sustainable sharing.

The "we" is formed in the primary physiological fusionality when this works; instead, it has to be rebuilt when that good fusionality was not sufficiently experienced, or repaired when it has been broken or traumatised.

In some cases, this may be a key part of our work: putting back together a basic "we" that coexists with the sense of individuality; always considering, though, this dynamic physiological alternating between the sense of individuality and otherness, on the one hand, and the healthy partial fusionality on the other.

The working alliance will then be one of the potential benefits of this physiological extension of the Self.

In conclusion, these five "minimalist" technical tools are in daily use, ubiquitous, and common to all analysts.

They deserve a mention despite their apparent aspecificity, since, like the house cat, they are part of our natural working day.

In my view, they can be understood theoretically through the invaluable conceptual legacy we received from Winnicott, the discoverer and best explorer of the area between Self and Not-Self.

References

Bollas, C. (1987). The unthought known. In: *The Shadow of the Object*. London: Free Association.
Bolognini, S. (1997a). "Empatia e patologie gravi". In: Correale, A. & Rinaldi, L. (a cura di) "Quale psicoanalisi per le psicosi?". Milan, Italy: Raffaello Cortina.
Bolognini, S. (1997b). Empathy and empathism. *International Journal of Psychoanalysis*, 78: 279–293.
Bolognini, S. (2002). *Psychoanalytic Empathy*. London: Free Association, 2004.
Bolognini, S. (2008). *Secret Passages: The Theory and Technique of Interpsychic Relations*. London: New Library of Psychoanalysis, Routledge, 2010.
Bolognini, S. (2014a). Interpsychique, intersubjectif, interpersonnel: états et passages. *Revue Psychosomatique*, 45: 143–161.
Bolognini, S. (2014b). Inauditum/Unerhoert!!!... Gewissen, Bewusstsein, Integration. Die Analyse als posttraumatische Erfahrung. In: I. Bozetti, I. Focke, & I. Hahn (Eds.), Unherhoert—Vom Hoeren un Verstehen. Stuttgart, Germany: Fachbuch Klett-Cotta.
Busch, F. (2014). *Creating a Psychoanalytic Mind: A Psychoanalytic Method and a Theory*. London: Routledge.
Fonda, P. (2000). La fusionalità e i rapporti oggettuali. *Rivista di Psicoanalisi*, 3: 429–449.
Green, A. (2000). The intrapsychic and intersubjective in psychoanalysis. *Psychoanalytic Quarterly*, 69: 1–39.
Greenberg, J. (2001). The analyst's participation: a new look. *Journal of the American Psychoanalytic Association*, 49(2): 359–381.
Greenson, R. R. (1954). Il suono mmm. In: *Esplorazioni psicoanalitiche*. Turin, Italy: Bollati Boringhieri, 1999.
Guss Teicholz, J. (1999). *Kohut, Loewald and the Postmoderns: a Comparative Study of Self and Relationship* (pp. 182–189). Hillsdale, NJ: Analytic Press.
Kaës, R. (1993). *Le groupe et le sujet du groupe*. Paris: Dunod.
Kaës, R., Faimberg, H., Enriquez, M., & Baranes, J. J. (1993). *Transmission de la vie psychique entre générations*. Paris: Dunod.
Losso, R. (2000). *Psicoanalisi della famiglia. Percorsi teorico-clinici*. Milan, Italy: Franco Angeli.
Losso, R. (2003). L'intrapsichico, l'interpersonale e il transpsichico nella psicoanalisi di coppia. *Relazione al Centro Psicoanalitico di Firenze*, January 30.
Micati, L. (1993). Quanta realtà può essere tollerata? *Rivista di Psicoanalisi*, 39: 153–163.

Segal, H. (1994). Phantasy and reality. In: *The Contemporary Kleinians of London*. New York: International Universities Press.
Widlöcher, D. (2003). La personne du psychanalyste et les processus d'empathie et de co-pensées. *Bulletin de la FEP, 57*: 89–95.
Winnicott, D. W. (1971). *Playing and Reality*. London: Tavistock/Routledge.
Yalom, I. (1970). *The Theory and Practice of Group Psychotherapy*. New York: Basic Books.

CHAPTER THREE

An investigation into the technical reasons Winnicott proposes that the analyst's objective hate towards the patient has to eventually be made available for interpretation

*Vincenzo Bonaminio and Paolo Fabozzi**

Our chapter is particularly focused on technical issues, not because we are only interested in technical issues in Winnicott— and we love Winnicott in a thorough-going way—but because he speaks to our hearts. We understand what he says differently from all the other authors. But we think that in the technical realm, Winnicott introduced revolutionary ideas without making too much propaganda about his revolution. His revolution is a quiet revolution but that makes a difference particularly in comparison to Melanie Klein's technique which at the time was very, very prevailing in the British Psychoanalytical Society. Just a note on the date, Melanie Klein (1946) wrote the first summary of her conclusion of the decade preceding in the famous paper, "Notes on Some Schizoid Mechanisms" in which she introduced fundamentally the concept of projective identification. It is very interesting that Winnicott, who at the time was interested in becoming, in being considered a Kleinian, produced in 1947 a paper like "Hate in the

---

*This is a longer version of the paper given by Vincenzo Bonaminio and Paolo Fabozzi (Rome) at the conference. It stems from our introduction for the third volume of the *Complete Works of D. W. Winnicott*. Special thanks go to Sara Nettleton who helped in the translation from Italian into English.

Countertransference", which is completely different from the ideas of Melanie Klein that he wanted to be part of. And the word "hate" is the first time in which a sentiment, a feeling, appeared in the psychoanalytical literature. So it's very provocative that such a sentiment burst out of the blue in the literature. There is a question: i.e., if Winnicott was aware of this, was he intentional in doing this or was he only being provocative.

Now we will stick to our intended text.

In his seminal paper "Hate in the Countertransference", Winnicott anticipates later developments in taking countertransference as a given, a realisation from his own clinical work. He describes ordinary countertransference as

> ... the identifications and tendencies belonging to an analyst's personal experience and personal development which provide the positive setting for his analytic work and make his work different in quality from that of any other analyst. (1947, p. 195)

This displaces the centre of gravity of psychoanalysis from the patient to the analyst but then his argument presents another emotional challenge. For some psychotic patients, analytic work cannot be completed unless the analyst has put his countertransference feelings at the disposal of the patient.

> This coincidence of love and hate to which I am referring is something distinct from the aggressive component complicating the primitive love impulse, and implies that in the history of the patient there was an environmental failure at the time of the first object-finding instinctual impulses.
>
> If the analyst is going to have crude feelings imputed to him he is best forewarned and so forearmed, for he must tolerate being placed in that position. Above all *he must not deny hate that really exists in himself. Hate that is justified in the present setting has to be sorted out and kept in storage and available for eventual interpretation.* (1947, p. 196, our emphasis)

That the analyst must offer something of himself to the patient was radical and unprecedented, and we might speculate that Winnicott's motive for choosing hate in this reversal of psychoanalytic perspective was partly a reaction to the neutrality previously attributed to the analyst's position.

His perspective demands a search for authenticity in the feelings of analyst and patient, an emphasis that echoes through his other works of that time. Later, in 1960, in "Ego Distortion in Terms of True and False Self" he again emphasised putting something of one's self at the disposal of the patient, an idea which reached its fullest elaboration in "The Use of an Object" (1968; see also Fabozzi, 2016).

"Hate in the Countertransference" was written one year after Klein's systematising paper, "Notes on Some Schizoid Mechanisms" (1946) which introduces the revolutionary concept of projective identification, and yet Winnicott seems uninterested in her theorisation, or takes it for granted, or disagrees with it. We think his progressive detachment from Klein's influence is being articulated here along with a different vision of psychoanalysis though he himself was probably not yet completely aware of it.

Where the crucial transition in Kleinian theory gives primacy to the conflictual dialectic between the libidinal drives and the aggressive impulses of the child in relation to the mother's breast, Winnicott does not conceptualise a primary aggression as an expression of the death drive or a reaction to frustration. Rather, he sees the roots of aggression as an expression of that "primitive […] motility potential" which has its origins in the first movements of the foetus within the womb. Although he does not explicitly mention the significance for the mother of these signs of life, this is essential because it is the mother who will see in the infant's earliest integration either erotic potential or signs of aggression.

Aggression is described through the fundamental developmental difference between the stages of concern and pre-concern. The aggressiveness of pre-concern is inherent in ruthless love. It does not embody an attack on the object, but the potential of motility in the processes of maturation. It is only when the child is firmly anchored in the stage of concern that aggressiveness is directed against the object.

Although aggression may appear primitive in states of profound narcissistic withdrawal, it is never primary; it is always the result of something that the object or the environment has done to the subject. Love and hate take shape within the continuous interplay between what is offered by the environment and the varyingly reactive responses of the individual.

His vision of the earliest stage of emotional development is based on his conviction that the analysis of psychotic, depressed, and hypochondriacal patients does not require a modification of Freudian technique—provided that "the transference situation inherent in such work" (p. 146) is taken into account.

Basing the study of primary development on the analyses of psychotic patients yields its greatest results in the identification and analysis of the processes in emotional development: integration (starting from a condition of primary normal un-integration); personalisation (the indwelling of the self in the body); and the assessment of spatial and temporal dimensions (the construction of the relationship with reality).

This conceptual organisation is highly innovative, as is the proposal that integration is a slow, gradual process as instinctual experiences are combined with maternal care. This is the first appearance of various Winnicottian leitmotifs: a) the establishment of an authentic relationship with external reality; b) the distinction and productive exchange between reality and fantasy; and c) the construction of the sense of being real.

Winnicott has yet to elaborate fully the contribution of the mother's psychic functioning to the baby's development, but he does outline it:

> In terms of baby and mother's breast (…) the baby has instinctual urges and predatory ideas. The mother has a breast and the power to produce milk, and the idea that she would like to be attacked by a hungry baby. These two phenomena do not come into relation with each other till the mother and child *live an experience together*. The mother being mature and physically able has to be the one with tolerance and understanding, so that it is she who produces a situation that may with luck result in the first tie the infant makes with an external object, an object that is external to the self from the infant's point of view (1945, p. 152, emphasis in the original).

He is preparing to construct a very specific situation: in presenting the baby with the breast, the mother must allow the baby to feel that he has created the experience himself.[1] The potential for this psychic function, fundamental to the relationship with external reality, lies in the possibility that an overlap may be created between something that stems from the mother's psyche and something that originates from the baby's nascent self.

Here too is the anticipation of other fundamental Winnicottian concepts: transitional objects and phenomena, the subjective object, and the intermediate area, that is, the potential space.

The idea that the mother "would like to be attacked by a hungry baby" makes the mother's psychic functioning central. But including the experience of the baby who encounters the mother's experience, Winnicott calls attention to the patient's experience (in the transference) and how it generates effects on the analyst's experience with the patient.

What unites the situations described in "Hate in the Countertransference" is that the object (mother/analyst) must face, and work through the reaction to "pressures" from the subject (the baby/patient). The technical implication—that the analyst must "bear strain"—opens up another unexplored field: the object's response to the subject's unconscious movements due to a tension that arises from primitive defensive processes.

Winnicott establishes a crucial connection when he states that the analyst "is in the position of the mother of an infant unborn or newly born" (p. 198). Every detail assumes a therapeutic value with patients "whose very early experiences have been so deficient or distorted that the analyst has to be the first in the patient's life to supply certain environmental essentials" (p. 198).

From these situations two issues arise that profoundly change the approach to psychoanalysis.

1. The patient's unconscious work on the analyst's unconscious, and thus on his mental functioning.
2. The functioning of the analyst's mind as a tool of psychoanalytic investigation.

The source of Winnicott's investigation of earliest infancy is his experience of transference situations encountered with psychotic patients. But his attention to the psychic relationship between mother and newborn enables him to grasp aspects of the transference–countertransference relationship, of the mental functioning of seriously ill patients, and of the origin of psychosis.

"Hate in the Countertransference" recognises the coexistence of three levels:

1. At the level of theory, he hypothesises that the mother's hate precedes that of the newborn. This dislodges the idea of an innate death drive.
2. From a clinical point of view he implies that for the psychotic patient to acquire the capacity to distinguish hate from love, he must first enter into contact with an object capable of feeling hate towards him.
3. Technically, he posits the coexistence of three forms of countertransference: a) one creates a blind spot; b) another constitutes the specific identity of that individual analyst; and c) a third, objective form exists in reaction to the personality of that particular patient.

The idea that Winnicott is engaged simply in magnifying the importance of the environment is clearly superficial and misleading. This is no mere introduction of the analyst's arbitrary subjectivity into the clinical situation. Instead, by combining the intrapsychic dimension with that of unconscious object relations it challenges both Freudian and Kleinian paradigms.

Actually the intersection of the above-mentioned three levels of countertransference, and their reciprocal interaction, produce a new theoretical-clinical picture of very early mental development, of pathological mental functioning, and of a consistent technique in which the analyst's unconscious is modified by the communications he receives from the patient's unconscious.

Both situations involve communication from unconscious to unconscious, each person tolerating and containing the emotions solicited by the other. However, there is also a more complex process at work: each unconscious has the capacity to modify the other in a continuous process of interpsychic construction, between subject and object (Fabozzi, 2012). This activates the psychic functions of the analyst or of the mother, enabling therapeutic work in the patient or the development of psychic functions in the neonate.

A fundamental link between aggression and the initiation of a relationship with external reality also represents a principal thread of research in the meanings of the transitional object, a concept with a monumental scope. The object coalesces from a Platonic ideal of representation to become a concrete object: something that can be manipulated, assisting the child's progressive attribution of meaning.

> The following complex statement has to be made. The infant can employ a transitional object when the internal object is alive and

real and good enough (not too persecutory). But this internal object depends for its qualities on the existence and aliveness and behaviour of the external object (breast, mother figure, general environmental care). (Winnicott, 1951, p. 237)

This is the revolutionary significance of the transitional object as "the first *not-me* possession", part of the child's emotional development, and that of the patient in analysis. Each term condenses further levels of experience.

"The first": the child creates a space where none existed before and which is invisible to an observer.

"Not-me": the differentiation between "me" and "not-me" represents the integration of the ego as a kind of opposition to the fundamental unity with the mother—an awareness of what it is not.

"Possession": an inseparable entanglement of aggression and libido as the basis for the birth of the relationship with the object.

In a letter to Money-Kyrle (November 27, 1952), Winnicott (cited in Rodman, 1987, p. 41) overtly declares to prefer the term "transitional" to "intermediate" because it evokes an intrinsic dynamism, implying that both object and space are in continual movement and development. So one of the principal functions of the transitional object is to act as a support for the toing and froing between the edges of internal and external worlds, between union and separation.

The newborn enters into a relation with the breast that was there, waiting to be discovered, and draws from it the sensation of having created it. The term "subjective object" conveys this from the baby's point of view. The baby experiences the breast in terms of an absence of separateness, deriving from it an experience of omnipotence. This is not a reformulation of primary narcissism since the presence and contribution of the object is crucial. The mother has a natural yet complex status as the supplier of the baby's need for both nourishment and illusion, and the capacity for illusion is created by her active adaptation to her baby. At first she will not make conscious or unconscious demands on him; she will respect his needs, emotional states, rhythms, and processes of maturation, so that he may discover the environment on the basis of his own spontaneous movements.

This is a mother of average predictability, not unstable, incoherent, or subject to exaggerated mood swings. In late pregnancy and during the early weeks of the baby's life she must be able to tolerate states of regression and complex identifications—with herself as a baby, with her own mother, and with her own child. The baby gradually establishes a relation to external reality through her gradual dis-adaptation from his needs, and assisted by the baby's discovery of a transitional object whose specific functions and meanings will enable him to recognise the external nature of objects.

It functions as a bridge: between child and mother at those points when the mother is absent; between the subjective object and the objective object; between what is internal and what is external. It is the first external object and it also represents the beginning of symbolism: it stands for the mother and, at the same time, for the Self of the child. What is crucial is its material quality and the environment must guarantee its psychic existence. In a sense, the gaze of the observer defines the nature of the transitional object in that the mother allows the child not to have to resolve whether the transitional object is created or found.

The transitional object can remain in a paradoxical space, a notional psychic place hitherto unexplored by psychoanalysis. When the child experiences separateness from the mother, a "me" that is distinct from "not-me", he can bridge the resulting distance with an experience that allows him to establish symbolically a new union with the mother. It involves the possibility of the child's creative gesture: a game, a movement towards the structuring of a symbol that will give form to a space that is always losing and regaining its potential character.

Giannakoulas and Hernandez (1997) suggest that the "limits" of potential space are constituted by four "dialectical dynamisms":

1. The mother's movements of identification with herself and with the newborn within the primary maternal preoccupation
2. The paradoxical nature of the transitional object
3. The mother's function as a mirror, which introduces elements of similarity and difference
4. The use of the object, where the child destroys the object just when it is on the point of becoming real, and then experiences its survival.

A circularity binds subject, object, and potential space allowing the dialectical movement between separation and union that is realised through playing and creativity.

It is perhaps too simplistic to say that the psychoanalytic process takes place within the same sort of transitional space. The space generated within the analytic relationship is not fixed but continually recreated by the reciprocal contribution of analyst and patient. Its topology is neither predictable nor prescribable and here the person of the analyst comes into play. If he is capable of grasping what the patient offers, embryonically and potentially, he will facilitate and contribute to the creation of an unforeseen and unforeseeable place within the analytic field.

This is not a posture deliberately chosen by the analyst. It is created unexpectedly, and to give life and form to the "play" between them, the analyst must be capable of grasping it and the patient of receiving it. It is crucial to Winnicott's "capacity to be alone" (1958), a concept that couples union and separateness, dependency and autonomy in the development of the child and in the analytic situation.

Clinical experience shows that the absence of this significant developmental step underlies a whole range of separation anxieties, panic attacks, and phobias, a vast spectrum of forms of psychopathology. During a panic attack, for example, the patient feels alone in facing the catastrophic threat of death because he has failed to establish the capacity to be alone in the presence of the other. Similarly, the claustro-agoraphobic patient feels lost in infinite space, like an astronaut who inadvertently severs the link to the spaceship and is left floating in the void.

For both Winnicott and Klein, these psychopathological dispositions are defences against the earliest anxieties but, unlike Klein, Winnicott defines this "falling for ever" (1962, p. 58; 1963,[2] p. 189) in terms of primitive agonies experienced by the infant when the environment does not fulfil its function of good enough holding.

In his theoretical-clinical thinking he explores a complex range of psychopathology attributable to specific forms of excess, intrusion, unpredictability, infiltration, and colonisation. When the environment, and in particular the mother's unconscious, subjects the child to these experiences, he will defend himself with well-organised, sophisticated defences that Winnicott defines at various levels.

This takes us further along a path, which is central and peculiar to his work. "Reparation in Respect of Mother's Organised Defence against Depression" (1948b) constitutes a landmark in this thinking and crystallises its innovative scope. Ground-breaking in its clinical observations, its density may account for its relative neglect,

> Early in my career a little boy came to hospital by himself and said to me "Please, Doctor, mother complains of a pain in my stomach,"

and this drew my attention usefully to the part mother can play. (1948b, p. 92)

Here Winnicott shows us a conception of the child's somatic illness as part of a structuring relation with the mother. Then he adds,

> Probably I get a specially clear view of this problem in a children's out-patient department because such a department is really a clinic for management of hypochondria in mothers [...] There is no sharp dividing line between the frank hypochondria of a depressed woman and a mother's genuine concern for a child. (p. 92)

Theoretically this radical assertion represents a decisive and explicit shift: the centre of gravity of psychology and psychopathology resides, not within the confines of the individual, but within the other who treats the child as an extension of itself. For Winnicott the child's self is not master in its own house,[3] as Freud wrote, in as much as it is occupied and colonised by the self of the mother. So the structuring relation with the mother as environment affects both the normal and the psychopathological development of the child. The clinician has to judge the shift from normality to pathology.

Despite using different theoretical models and idioms, Anna Freud, Klein, and Winnicott all pursue what are in many respects convergent lines of thinking, all guided by clinical practice.

Winnicott reformulates the issue in a radically different way in his essay "Paediatrics and Psychiatry" (1948a). Without explicitly mentioning Klein he asserts:

> It has often been said to me: the idea that mad people are like babies, or small children, simply isn't true. Can I make it clear that I do not suggest that the insane are behaving like infants any more than that neurotics are just like older children. Ordinary healthy children are not neurotic (though they can be) and ordinary babies are not mad. (p. 159)

In fact this thinking originates well before 1948. It is implied in "The Manic Defence" (1935) where Winnicott describes the manic defence as the denial (Freud's *Verleugnung*) of internal reality, of the sensations related to depression and suspended animation. This implies a basic dissociation within the personality, an idea he was to develop ten years later (1945) through the concept of "integration and non-integration", which would later lead him, in "Ego Distortion in Terms of True and False Self" (1960), to a final definition of "the dissociation in internal reality".

A basic dissociation in personality is not the same as repression or splitting, both of which imply an ego to do the work. Rather the child's further development is foreclosed if the integration facilitated by the environment cannot be made or is blocked: "Only after integration-the child starts to have a self" (Winnicott, 1955, p. 153).

In "Reparation in Respect of Mother's Organised Defence against Depression" (1948b), Winnicott refers to the "false reparation" we meet in clinical practice. It is false because it occurs in relation, not to the patient's guilt, but to the external other. This theory leads to his clinical discoveries concerning dissociation in connection with the false self (1960), but the central core of the configuration has a more comprehensive relevance, capable of explaining, along a continuum, both primitive psychopathological phenomena in the early structuring of the self, and the later schizoid phenomena with which Winnicott's concept of dissociation was initially associated.

At the beginning of the 1948 paper Winnicott writes:

> This false reparation appears through the *patient's identification with his mother* and the dominating factor is not the patient's own guilt but the mother's organized defence against depression and unconscious guilt. (1948, p. 91, our emphasis)
>
> (…) the depression of the child can be the mother's depression in reflection. [He] uses the mother's depression as an escape from his or her own; this provides a false restitution and reparation in relation to the mother, and this hampers the development of a personal restitution capacity (…). It will be seen that these children, in extreme cases, have *a task which can never be accomplished*. Their task is first *to deal with the mother's mood*. If they succeed in the immediate task, they do no more than succeed in creating an atmosphere in which they can *start on their own lives*. (p. 93, our emphasis except for the last sentence where emphasis was in the original)

Here Winnicott is starting to describe the "psychic work" done on behalf of the other within the self, through identification. At its most extreme it may extend to occupation of the self by the other (Bonaminio & Di Renzo, 2000).

Close to the end of his scientific career, Winnicott concludes the journey begun with "Hate in the Countertransference", in an undervalued 1967 paper, "The Aetiology of Infantile Schizophrenia in Terms of Adaptive Failure" where he discusses the aetiological factors proposed by his theory of emotional development, which include the "mother's capacity to adapt to the infant's needs through her healthy ability to identify with the baby". He notes:

> It seems necessary to add to this the concept of the mother's unconscious (repressed) hate of the child. Parents naturally love and hate their babies in varying degrees. This does not do damage. At all ages, and in earlier infancy especially, the effect of the repressed death wish towards the baby is harmful, and it is beyond the baby's capacity to deal with this. At a later stage than this one that concerns us here, one can see a child all the time making efforts *in order to arrive at the starting post*—that is, to counteract the parents' unconscious wish (covered by reaction formation) that the child should be dead. (1967, pp. 221–222, emphasis in the original)

The child's effort to arrive at the starting post by managing the occupation of the potential self by the parents' unconscious hampers the development of personal capacities. This is similar to the task of the depressed child in dealing with the mother's moods in order to create an atmosphere in which he can begin "a life of his own".

Notes

1. "I think of the process as if two lines came from opposite directions, liable to come near each other. If they overlap there is a moment of *illusion*—a bit of experience which the infant can take as *either* his hallucination *or* a thing belonging to external reality" (1945, p. 152, emphasis in the original).
2. The date of this paper, "Fear of Breakdown" is uncertain. The editors of Winnicott's posthumous *Psychoanalytic Explorations* (London: Karnac, 1989) are prone to dating this seminal essay to 1963, but they, then, insert a question mark after the date to emphasise the uncertainty of timing. The date of 1974 is generally given to this essay in the majority of reference lists.

3. Freud had already epitomised this concept in his most famous sentence, "The ego is not master in its own house" (1917a, p. 142).

References

Bonaminio, V., & Di Renzo, M. (2000). ... A task which can never be accomplished ... to deal with mother's mood. Winnicott's clinical conception of the individual's psychic work done for the other. Paper for the Congress on Winnicott's thought: "Winnicott and Psychoanalysis", Milan. In press, 2017.

Bonaminio, V., & Fabozzi, P. (2017). Introduction to Volume Three (1946–1951) of *The Collected Works of D. W. Winnicott (1896–1971)*. Oxford: Oxford University Press.

Fabozzi, P. (2012). A silent yet radical future revolution: Winnicott's innovative perspective. *Psychoanalytic Quarterly, 81*: 601–626.

Fabozzi, P. (2016). The use of the analyst and the sense of being real: the clinical meaning of Winnicott's "The use of an object". *Psychoanalytic Quarterly, 85*: 1–34.

Freud, S. (1917a). A difficulty in the path of psycho-analysis. *S. E., 17*. London: Hogarth.

Giannakoulas, A., & Hernandez, M. (1997). On the construction of potential space. In: M. Bertolini, A. Giannakoulas, & M. Hernandez (Eds.), *Squiggles and Spaces. Volume 1: Revisiting the Work of D. W. Winnicott*. London: Whurr, 2001.

Klein, M. (1946). Notes on some schizoid mechanisms. In: Klein, M., Heimann, P., Isaacs, S., & Riviere, J., *Developments in Psychoanalysis*. London: Hogarth and the Institute of Psychoanalysis, 1952.

Rodman, F. (1987). *The Spontaneous Gesture: Selected Letters of D. W. Winnicott*. Cambridge, MA: Harvard University Press.

Winnicott, D. W. (1935). The manic defence. In: *Through Paediatrics to Psychoanalysis. Collected Papers*. Hogarth and the Institute of Psychoanalysis, 1958.

Winnicott, D. W. (1945). Primitive emotional development. In: *Through Paediatrics to Psychoanalysis. Collected Papers*. Hogarth and the Institute of Psychoanalysis, 1958.

Winnicott, D. W. (1947). Hate in the countertransference. In: *Through Paediatrics to Psychoanalysis. Collected Papers*. Hogarth and the Institute of Psychoanalysis, 1958.

Winnicott, D. W. (1948a). Paediatrics and psychiatry. In: *Through Paediatrics to Psychoanalysis. Collected Papers*. Hogarth and the Institute of Psychoanalysis, 1958.

Winnicott, D. W. (1948b). Reparation in respect of mother's organised defence against depression. In: *Through Paediatrics to Psychoanalysis. Collected Papers*. Hogarth and the Institute of Psychoanalysis, 1958.

Winnicott, D. W. (1951). Transitional objects and transitional phenomena. In: *Through Paediatrics to Psychoanalysis. Collected Papers*. Hogarth and the Institute of Psychoanalysis, 1958.

Winnicott, D. W. (1955). Group influences and the maladjusted child: the school aspect. In: *The Family and Individual Development*. London: Tavistock, 1965.

Winnicott, D. W. (1958). The capacity to be alone. In: *The Maturational Processes and the Facilitating Environment. Studies in the Theory of Emotional Development*. London: Hogarth and the Institute of Psychoanalysis, 1965.

Winnicott, D. W. (1960). Ego distortion in terms of true and false Self. In: *The Maturational Processes and the Facilitating Environment. Studies in the Theory of Emotional Development*. London: Hogarth and the Institute of Psychoanalysis, 1965.

Winnicott, D. W. (1962). Ego integration in child development. In: *The Maturational Processes and the Facilitating Environment. Studies in the Theory of Emotional Development*. London: Hogarth and the Institute of Psychoanalysis, 1965.

Winnicott, D. W. (1963). Fear of breakdown. In: *Psychoanalytic Explorations*. London, Karnac, 1989.

Winnicott, D. W. (1967). The aetiology of infantile schizophrenia in terms of adaptive failures. In: *Thinking about Children*. London: Karnac, 1996.

Winnicott, D. W. (1968). The use of an object and relating through identifications. In: *Psychoanalytic Explorations*. London: Karnac, 1989.

CHAPTER FOUR

Meeting Winnicott

Juliet Hopkins

I first met Dr Winnicott in 1960 when I had the opportunity to observe him performing "snack-bar therapy". This was his name for the provision of the least help needed to release a child from an impasse in development. Winnicott did this work in his role as child psychiatrist at Paddington Green Hospital. On the day that I visited, the last child patient was what was then called "an illegitimate child", a boy of seven years who was brought by his voluble Irish mother. When the interview with Winnicott was over the boy ran off to the toilet. As he emerged to rejoin his mother I was amazed to see Winnicott stand up and bar his way. I was still more amazed when, in a flash, the boy climbed straight up Winnicott, slithered over his shoulder and ran to his mother's arms. We all laughed and Winnicott said something about the boy's courage standing him in good stead.

Winnicott's playful use of an oedipal challenge to this fatherless boy was a startling contrast to the exclusively interpretative approach to which I'd been introduced at the Tavistock Clinic. As students of child psychotherapy we were not expected in those days to initiate play with children. Perhaps Winnicott enjoyed having presented an unorthodox challenge to me as well as to his small patient.

In 1961 I was fortunate to have Winnicott as the supervisor of my youngest training case. I felt overawed when he agreed to see me. My anxiety increased when he fixed a regular appointment at lunchtime and sat with a cup of coffee and a cigarette listening to me with closed eyes. I felt sure he would have preferred an after-dinner nap. However, when he shared his thoughts I found he had not been asleep but had been listening intently. There was nothing doctrinal about his views. He never advised me what to do or say. He opened his eyes to share his thoughts, letting me see how he played freely with alternative ideas and encouraged me to do the same. I learned to tolerate much uncertainty.

Thirty years later I wrote a paper describing how Winnicott's supervision enabled me to facilitate the development of my little patient who could not play. Now I want to introduce Lynne Murray's chapter by selecting only those aspects of this child's early development in therapy which concerned play themes normally belonging within the first two years of life, the years with which Lynne is centrally concerned.

My patient was a little boy of three years old called Paddy. He had no speech and was not toilet-trained. His parents reported that he often wandered off and got lost. He showed no awareness of danger and regularly ate dirt and rubbish. He had never learned to play but simply wandered about "getting into things". Paddy's birth and early history had been normal but his development was so slow and so deviant that the referring paediatrician was uncertain whether he was mentally handicapped or psychotic. Today I would give him a Winnicottian diagnosis and say he was a child whose spontaneous gesture had never been recognised.

Paddy was an only child. His mother was a seriously depressed and anxious woman, preoccupied with thoughts of suicide. Paddy's father was a very eccentric man who had never been able to find a job. Neither parent had ever thought of playing with Paddy and they were at a loss to know how to relate to him. Fortunately, they were eager for help and attended the clinic weekly while I saw Paddy five times a week, the frequency expected at that time.

My first encounters with Paddy were utterly bewildering. He wandered cheerfully around the room, clambered over furniture, dropped and threw toys, and made a lot of noise by banging and shouting. I found myself entirely unable to think of any of the interpretations I had been learning how to give. However, in supervision Winnicott warmly supported my intuitive response which was simply to verbalise what

Paddy was doing and feeling. Winnicott spoke of the importance for children of naming their emotions, intentions, and body parts. Naming, he said, makes shared and therefore socially acceptable what previously was only private fantasy. Putting children's experiences into words gives them greater self-awareness and hence greater control: it allows fantasy to be checked with reality, it increases the capacity to remember, and it reduces guilt. So "naming" was not simply the failure to interpret which I had feared it to be.

Fortunately, Paddy warmly welcomed my attempts to feed back in words what he was feeling and doing. He began to look eagerly at my face to see my interest in him reflected there. Much later, in a paper on the "mirror-role of mother" (1971), Winnicott described how vital it is for the infant to see his mother's face reflecting and responding to his own state of mind, not frozen or preoccupied. Paddy appreciated that my face and words mirrored his experience and so confirmed his existence. He began to talk, to point to himself when he wanted something, and to call himself "Paddy". He seemed touchingly overjoyed to discover that he possessed his own thoughts and feelings. He had arrived at feeling "I am".

For Paddy, the discovery of "I am" was accompanied by the parallel exploration of "We are". Paddy took great pleasure in having or doing the same as me. He was thrilled to discover that we both had blue sweaters, both had buttons, and could both draw circles. He liked to imitate me and be imitated. We "clapped handies", made animal noises, and played peek-a-boo. Thus we established mother–baby games which normally originate within the first year. Winnicott thought these games expressed a mutual identification in which Paddy retained through play the potential for assuming either the mother or the baby role. He thought that such early playfulness took place in the transitional space at a time when the baby was not yet fully aware of the mother as a separate person upon whom he depended. Certainly at this early stage of his therapy, Paddy had not yet begun to experience me as a separate person whom he missed between sessions or whom he could imagine to have a personal life of my own.

I remember asking Winnicott how I could enable Paddy to move on to the next stage of development; surely interpretation was needed now? But no, it seemed that one form of playing could lead spontaneously to another. Playing could be both a reflection of the therapeutic process and a means of bringing it about. Paddy began to pretend. His first pretend play, like that of many babies, took the form of pretending to feed me and inviting me to pretend to feed him. Plasticine and water became "nanas and mook" (bananas and milk) and part of each daily session became a mutual feast.

Winnicott explained that this new capacity for togetherness was essential for providing the context in which Paddy could risk discriminating and tolerating differences. Indeed, Paddy soon became interested in observing and exploring my body and focused on differences in our clothing and anatomy instead of on our similarities. All the toys had previously been held in common, but now he selected "his" cars and bricks and allotted me the others. The difference between "me" and "not-me" was becoming increasingly delineated.

During this period Paddy gradually developed an attachment to me. He greeted me with enthusiasm and felt very rejected when it was time to go. Disillusionment was painful. He was forced to confront my separateness and to face his anger about it. Hide and seek became his favourite game. He would jump out of his hiding place to frighten me and liked to kick me on occasions. I was becoming for him both a mental image which he could recall in my absence and a separate person in the outside world who merited both love and hate.

During my supervision I gradually realised that Winnicott's approach to children's play was different from Melanie Klein's. Klein used play to understand and interpret children's anxieties. Winnicott did this too, but he was more interested in the way that children themselves use play to reflect and facilitate the development of the self. Winnicott recognised that, through playing, therapy of a deep-going kind may be done without interpretative work. So it was with Paddy, who now moved forward into fully symbolic play, play that typically begins in the third year. He intended that we should both enact fierce crocodiles.

It's at this point, when interpretation began to play a part, that I must leave you. Ten years after my supervision Winnicott published *Playing and Reality* and I hoped that Paddy had contributed to this formulation of his ideas.

Reference

Winnicott, D. W. (1967). Mirror-role of mother and family in child development. In: *Playing and Reality* (pp. 111–118). London: Tavistock, 1971.

CHAPTER FIVE

There's no such thing as a baby: how relationships support development from birth to two

Lynne Murray

In 1985, the Winnicott Trust, chaired by Martin James, established a research fellowship at the University of Cambridge. The fellowship was attached to the Department of Paediatrics, at that time headed up by John Davis, and the Child Care and Development Group, led by Martin Richards. The purpose of the fellowship was to look in an empirical way at some of Winnicott's ideas, and in particular to conduct research on the role of babies' early relationships in their longer term development. I was honoured to be appointed as the Winnicott Fellow. I had used Winnicott's thinking throughout my work with Colwyn Trevarthen in Edinburgh, and had become interested in the effects of maternal depression in the postnatal months on babies' development. The Winnicott Fellowship enabled me to start up what has developed into a long-term study of the development of children of depressed and well mothers, one lasting through to the children's twenty-second year. This presentation includes the fruits of that fellowship work, as well as a broader look at what research has revealed about "ordinary" parenting on child development, and it ends with an account of how, together with my colleagues, I have been able to take the basic scientific work forward to inform interventions with parents living in conditions of extreme socio-economic adversity. Much of the research described in this chapter is presented in greater detail, with full references, in my book *The Psychology of Babies: How Relationships Support Development from Birth to Two*, published in 2014 by Constable & Robinson. Work that is not included in this book is referenced separately.

As Winnicott said, "There is no such thing as a baby" … without, that is, the care they receive. Indeed, babies are entirely dependent on others for their survival and development. To make sure they receive the care they need, babies therefore quickly need to get into relationship with people who will be committed to them. Research over the last twenty years has shown how both babies and adults are geared up for this to happen. Experiments with adults have shown, for example, how the "cute" features characteristic of baby faces—the chubby cheeks, broad forehead, and wide set large eyes positioned half way down the face—contribute to our perception of how endearing they are, not only in human babies, but also in puppies, kittens, baby seals, and chicks. If photographs of these typical baby faces are morphed to become narrower, they lose some of their "babyishness" quality, and we perceive them as less cute and attractive.

In line with these findings, research using brain scanning and activation techniques has shown that when we see a baby, rather than an adult face, specific parts of the brain are activated, with these responses being stronger for our own, rather than an unfamiliar, baby. These responses happen within a fraction of a second, and occur in those parts of the brain that are associated with feelings of reward, and that involve the hormone oxytocin, well known to be implicated in feelings of attachment and empathy. These special brain responses to babies are matched by our behaviour—when we engage with a young baby, we typically place our face at just the distance that allows the baby to see us clearly; we use a specialised kind of speech—"baby talk"—that is particularly attractive to babies, with its high pitch, melodic contours, and short utterances; and if the baby starts to look towards us, we show a number of stereotyped behaviours, like flashing our eyebrows, and opening our eyes wide in a "greeting" response that attracts the baby's attention and facilitates his (or her, of course) engagement.

Just as adults are ready to respond to babies, so babies are ready to respond to other people. Even from birth, babies prefer to look at a face-like form rather than a scrambled up version; and they prefer faces that signal readiness to engage with them—that is, faces with open, as opposed to shut eyes, and eyes that face forward rather than to the side.

These basic preferences all help to get the baby engaged in relationships with others. But preferences for the people who are involved in the baby's care, rather than people in general, also develop rapidly, with the mother's voice, face, and smell all being preferred to those of another, unfamiliar, woman within just days of birth. And when the baby shows this preference, for example by turning to the mother when she speaks, or snuggling in to her to catch her odour, it can be an intensely rewarding demonstration to the parent of how special she is for her baby, and this helps in the process of feeling in intimate relationship with him. One of the most dramatic signs of the baby's ability to be in relationship with other people is the imitation of another person's facial gestures, like tongue protrusion or mouth opening. This can best be observed when the baby is in a quiet, alert state, without distractions, and when the adult performs the action to be imitated clearly in a sequence of demonstrations. It is a remarkable ability when one considers that the baby has never seen his reflection in a mirror—he must, in some basic sense, connect up the sight of someone else's movements with his own experience of feeling the same movements, an experience that has been seen as a fundamental building block of empathy.

Although the biological preparedness of both babies and parents helps us get into relationship with each other, it is of course the case that relationships between babies and their carers vary markedly. This variability is critical, since parents have to bring up their babies in a wide range of environments that place different demands on them. Cross-cultural studies of parenting are extremely useful in identifying what are more "universal" behaviours, and which can vary without babies ceasing to develop well. It is also important to study variations in parenting and child development within a given culture, as this can help us understand which aspects of what we do as parents can best support a child's development, as this can help us to support parents who may be experiencing difficulties.

Over the past decades, several longitudinal studies have been conducted in the UK which have involved both typical populations and also those experiencing particular kinds of difficulty, such as the parent's experience of depression. One of the main lessons to be learned from such research is that our old concept of "sensitive" parenting needs to be far more refined, so that we can identify the specific ingredients of which aspects of what parents do are most important for different kinds of development. This conclusion also has important implications for how we conduct observations of parents and their babies. In the past, studies have typically asked parents simply to play with their babies when the babies are contented, either in face-to-face interactions without objects, or with toys. Yet we know now that observations in these rather bland contexts are not as informative as we would like, and that in order to understand the specific aspects of parenting that are important to different child outcomes, we also need to think about the specific observational frames that we use to elucidate what is happening. This appreciation of specificity is not only of general importance, but it could be particularly useful for framing how clinical observations are conducted, and even the content of interventions.

This specificity of effects of parenting can be illustrated by considering different domains of child development, and it can be convenient to divide them up into the following grouping: i) social understanding; ii) emotion regulation and self-control; iii) secure attachment; iv) cognitive development. In each of these areas, the child's development by age two is a good predictor of his future development, and so if parents can give the kind of support in each domain that is important for the child to flourish early on, it is also likely to have longer-term benefits.

Social understanding

Very important developments in social understanding take place over the first two years. These include an *implicit* sense of others' experience and the capacity to realise that other people can have a different experience of the world from our own. This capacity is referred to as having a "theory of mind", and is gradually developed as a conscious, explicit knowledge of others' mental states from around three years of age. A second, and closely related ability developing within the first two years, is to be able to cooperate with other people. Third, babies, at least in cultures such as the UK and US, start to recognise their reflection in a mirror as being an image of themselves.

Research has shown that a number of specific parenting techniques support these developments. Cross-cultural studies have shown, for example, that differences in parents' mirroring, or imitation, of their babies' social expressions in the first few months' lead to differences between cultures in the rates of mirror self-recognition. Thus, in societies where affiliation, rather than individuation, is valued, parents do not tend to show the same level of facial or vocal imitation of the baby's communicative signals, and instead use touch to respond to the baby—although the overall level of their responsiveness is similar. In turn, this lower rate of parents' picking up and mirroring back the baby's cues in the early months predicts less awareness in the child of his identity in the mirror later on, suggesting a less individuated sense of himself.

Other parenting practices that influence social understanding are engaging in "pretend" play. Thus, games where the parent helps the baby to think about others' experiences, for example, in a pretend tea party in which the baby can be invited to wonder whether the teddy is hungry, or whether the toy sausages might still be too hot for him to eat, have been found to predict better "theory of mind" abilities. Parents' simply talking about mental states and feelings in everyday conversations also helps children develop the ability to understand other people and their feelings. One particularly good opportunity for this kind of talk is when sharing picture books if the content is suitable (that is, it features characters having different experiences and feelings). In fact, studies have shown that parents are more likely to talk about mental states and emotions when sharing picture books with their small children than in other contexts, and that such talk is a good predictor of children's later theory of mind and social relationships.

Emotion regulation and self-control

Acquiring the ability to manage difficult emotions and exercise self-control is one of the greatest challenges for children in their first two years. There are of course important individual differences in children's temperament that influence this process. Some babies, although healthy, are more reactive than others, and respond with distress to even slight changes in what goes on, and they take longer, and require more support, to become settled and calm. This can make caring for them more taxing, and parents of such babies are in particular need of support themselves. However, in addition to the impact of the baby's own individual characteristics, parents can make a difference to how well the child becomes able to manage his difficult feelings. This is particularly relevant to managing feelings of aggression, but also to normal developmental challenges, such as managing to get off to sleep without a lot of difficulty, and without requiring a great deal of parental support.

With regard to aggression, humans are typically at their most aggressive around the age of two, as the phrase the "terrible two's" suggests.

In the majority of children, the level of aggression gradually reduces over time from around the ages of two to three, as they develop more effective strategies to handle feelings of frustration and anger. In a minority, however, aggressive behaviour becomes established in a pervasive and persistent pattern (that is, the child will frequently be angry in a wide range of situations, and this behaviour persists over time), and longitudinal studies have shown that if this is the case, the chances that the child will develop significant problems with violent and antisocial behaviour in later life are very much increased. This is why it is of particular clinical, and societal, importance to try to support parents whose children may be developing these aggressive tendencies in the early years, before the child's behaviour becomes entrenched and more difficult to change.

As with the development of social understanding, longitudinal studies have shown that a number of specific aspects of parenting make the development of emotion regulation difficulties and of pervasive and persistent aggression problems less likely. In the early weeks, as Winnicott described, parental physical holding, including rocking, patting, stroking, and close containment, is the most appropriate way of supporting a baby in distress; increasingly, research shows that these behaviours have the effect of reducing the baby's physiological stress. As the baby develops, however, there are more opportunities for parents to support the baby's own capacities to deal with difficulties. Even in the first weeks, babies can turn their head, or cut their gaze, in order to reduce the impact of incoming stimulation; or they may be able to suck on their own fists to help soothe themselves. One facet of early social interactions that may be particularly effective in helping babies to develop their emotion regulation capacities has been highlighted by Ed Tronick and his colleagues, and is termed the "mismatch-repair" process. Like Winnicott, Tronick draws attention to the fact that parental responsiveness is not perfect, and indeed, that being "good-enough", rather than perfect, has important advantages for the baby. For example, the parent who slightly overshoots and does something that mildly surprises the three month old during a social interaction, may interrupt the baby's engagement and cause him to cut his gaze. Such signals, if noticed by parents, can help them tailor the level of stimulation they then offer to the baby a few moments later, so that it is more manageable and does not exceed the baby's capacities to tolerate what is happening. In this way, the difficult moment is "repaired", and the baby gains the experience that things can go slightly wrong, but can get back on track rather than having catastrophic consequences, and thereby begin to build up a sense of being able to handle disruptions. Indeed, babies whose parents are able to support them with such "repairs" to the normal misattunements that inevitably occur during social interactions then show less difficulty in handling more significant challenges.

Later in development, the playful interactions between babies and their parents typically become more boisterous, with "rough and tumble" and "play fighting" games being more common, particularly though the second year. These give babies the opportunity to experience "scary" feelings within the containment of a safe affectionate relationship, and at a stage when the babies are developing what Winnicott called "the capacity for concern", they are able to learn more about their potentially aggressive feelings and how to manage them without harming their parent. Studies show that when babies can experience this kind of play, it can benefit their relationships with other children, helping them to manage aggression in this context too.

Much evidence has shown that the way in which parents handle conflict situations is of great importance in preventing the baby's normal aggression becoming settled into a difficult pattern of response to challenges. One principle is consistency: if the parent at first says "no" to the baby's angry demand for something, and then relents when the baby's anger escalates, this simply encourages the baby's aggressive demands and leaves them uncontained. Similarly, if the parent attempts to do something with the baby that causes an angry response, and the parent then gives up trying, this again may encourage the baby's anger. On the other hand, if parents can be consistent in a way that is not authoritarian, that is, imposing their will by harsh, forceful means, but rather achieve a balance of being firm but warm, child aggressive behaviour problems are less likely to develop.

On the positive side, provision of containing routines can help babies feel that their world is reliable, and this can help them tolerate frustrations and delays, since they will have built up a sense that what they need will be provided. Further, when parents can capitalise on the baby's growing social understanding through the second year, and find ways in which to support the baby's desire to share experiences in cooperative activities when he can derive satisfaction and pride from being helpful, even in small ways, this can build up benign, rather than difficult, cycles of relating where child aggressive behaviour is less likely to be fostered.

Although many of the parenting practices that are relevant to aggression are particularly clear throughout the second year, difficult patterns of relating that can lead to such problems can be evident in the early months. This is especially likely in clinical contexts such as parental depression, where the irritability and anger that sometimes accompanies depression can spill over into early mother–baby contacts. We found, for example, that postnatally depressed mothers were more likely to express hostility towards their infants, particularly males, even at two months post-partum. While this did not appear to affect the babies' responses to other people at this time, by four months these babies had become more emotionally dysregulated, a pattern that persisted and in turn provoked increased maternal negativity, such that by five years a vicious cycle of negative, coercive parenting, together with child conduct problems had developed (Morrell & Murray, 2003).

The development of secure attachment

The period from around six months, when babies become more aware of their dependency on those who care for them, through to two years, is when babies typically develop strong feelings of attachment to particular individuals. Attachment theory was developed by John Bowlby and his colleague Mary Ainsworth, complementing the insights of Winnicott on the earlier parent-child relationship. Since Bowlby and Ainsworth's initial work, a large volume of research has been devoted to both the precursors and the consequences of the different kinds of attachment that babies develop over their first two years. The main distinction is that made between babies who are "securely" attached to the person who cares for them, and those who are "insecurely" attached, with secure attachment referring to relationships where the baby has grown to trust that the carer will be both available when needed, and will also respond to his needs in a caring and sensitive way. This kind of parental responsiveness is particularly important for the development of a secure attachment in situations where the baby feels vulnerable, for example, when he is ill, tired, frightened, or distressed—and this is one of the main reasons why simply observing a baby and the carer together in a happy play situation may not be very informative. Studies have also shown that aside from *behaving* sensitively to the baby's needs in distressing circumstances, the parent's ability to show the baby or young child that they *understand* how he feels is important for secure attachments to develop, a capacity sometimes referred to as "reflective functioning".

Of all the developments in infant behaviour studied in the first two years, attachment quality is one of the strongest predictors of later adjustment, and it is particularly relevant to the older child's, adolescent's, and even adult's close, intimate relationships. Some research has also found that the lack of a secure attachment in late infancy can pose a risk for the development of affective disorder. Our own research showed, for example, that babies of postnatally depressed mothers, who can find it hard to respond to their needs, had a greater risk of developing an insecure attachment, and that this in turn predicted a lack of "ego resilience" in early childhood, and greater risk of depression in adolescence (Murray et al., 2011).

Cognitive development

Just as each of the three domains of development outlined above is facilitated by specific kinds of parental care, so the baby's cognitive development is more likely to flourish where particular kinds of support are available. In fact, babies do much to push their own cognitive development forward, and they work at exploring the links between their own actions and what happens in the world around them from a very early age. Sensing these "contingencies" between their own actions and external events is a basic building block of learning abilities. Nevertheless, one of the best sources of contingent information for babies comes in the form of other people's social responses to them. Even in early face-to-face interactions, parents' responses to their babies' social cues are important, and many studies have found that when parents are responsive, babies are better able to learn the links between their own actions and other events. The impact of parents' responsiveness is well demonstrated in studies that experimentally disrupt it—for example, when parents are asked to stop responding and instead adopt a still face, or when their responses are made non-contingent by use of their being relayed to the baby in a non-live closed loop video sequence. These studies show that babies' attention and affect are very quickly disturbed by such disruptions, and they typically become withdrawn from their environment and self-absorbed.

Aside from the early patterns of contingent face-to-face responsiveness, parents continue to support their babies' cognitive development with specific forms of support. A key behaviour that has been the focus of much research is "scaffolding". This refers to the parent's ability to facilitate the baby's exploration and mastery of the world by providing support pitched just at the limits of the baby's capacity in a way that allows him to progress to the next step. It could involve something as simple as steadying a brick at an angle so that the baby can succeed in pushing it into a hole in a shape sorter. A particularly good way of supporting cognitive development, and especially language, is through sensitive "book-sharing". In this context, as noted above, parents tend to speak in special ways, and as well as talking more about emotions and mental states, they simply name and label things more, and expand on what is happening. So effective has book-sharing been found to be, that it has been called "a language acquisition device".

If parents are unable to provide the kind of input described above, and their interactions with the baby are disrupted, for example, by clinical conditions such as depression, with its accompanying self-preoccupation that makes responding to the baby's cues difficult, then the impact on babies' cognitive development can be far-reaching. We found, for example, that boy babies of depressed mothers were likely to experience particularly low levels of responsiveness during interactions in the first few months (Murray, Kempton, Woolgar, & Hooper, 1993), and these difficulties were predictive of poorer IQ scores in late infancy, which in turn were associated with poorer GCSE results at age sixteen years (Murray et al., 2010).

Clinical implications

Given all the evidence on what specific kinds of parenting support are most likely to facilitate different aspects of babies' development, it is now possible to devise more targeted interventions. Although Winnicott felt that "you can't teach a mother how to hold her baby", he did see the importance of supporting parents so that their natural capacities for caring for their babies could be expressed. Our work with a deprived population living in the peri-urban settlement, Khayelitsha, outside Cape Town in South Africa, follows this approach. We had found, in earlier epidemiological work, that parents living in conditions of significant social and economic adversity had high rates of depression, and their interactions with their infants were often intrusive and insensitive;

correspondingly, rates of secure attachment in their babies were low (Cooper et al., 1999; Tomlinson, Cooper, & Murray, 2005). Accordingly, we mounted a home visiting intervention, delivered by trained women from the local community, that provided counselling support to parents from late pregnancy through the first six months. As well as counselling, parents received support with their relationships with their infants, and in particular help with understanding their babies' social cues and with managing difficult, distressed infant behaviour. In effect, the intervention targeted the main sources of insecure attachment. At the end of the intervention, as well as at follow-up when the babies were one year old, those parents who had received the home visiting were, as we had hoped, more sensitive and less intrusive than parents who had not received it; and at eighteen months, the babies in the intervention group were more likely to be securely attached (Cooper et al., 2009).

While the results of this home visiting support were encouraging, and of potential importance for the children's longer term socio-emotional development, we found not all areas of their functioning showed a benefit of the intervention. Thus, when we measured the children's cognitive performance, using the Mental Development Index of the Bayley Scales, we found almost no difference between the scores of infants whose mothers received support and those whose mothers had not. Further, we found no association at all between the children's security of attachment and their cognitive performance (Murray, Cooper, Arteche, Stein, & Tomlinson, 2016a). This is important, as the level of cognitive development, in terms of school achievement and literacy, is very poor in South Africa, even compared to other low income countries, and there is an urgent need to improve the situation in order to help break cycles of disadvantage. With this in mind, we therefore decided to develop a further intervention that was specifically targeted at supporting children's cognition and language. As noted before, book-sharing is one means by which parents can do much to help their child's development, particularly in relation to language and pre-literacy skills. Accordingly we mounted a book-sharing training programme, also based in Khayelitsha, and we similarly trained and employed local women to deliver it. The training comprised parents meeting in small groups once a week over a period of eight weeks. On each occasion the parents would receive a presentation from the trainer in the form of a PowerPoint, illustrating the principles of good book-sharing practice, each week based around a particular book. The principal focus was to support parents to follow their baby's interests and facilitate his engagement with the book, talking around the picture content and linking it to their child's own experience. After every group session, each parent received about ten minutes of one-to-one support from the trainer. They then took the "book of the week" home, and were encouraged to try to share it with their baby for ten minutes a day. After eight weeks, we compared parents and babies who had received the training with those who had not. We found that the trained parents had become far more sensitive to their babies during book-sharing, and they also engaged their babies in reciprocal interactions around the book. Their babies had also made big improvements in their attention span and in their language development over the same period, and these gains were related to the changes in their parents' interactions with them; we also found some evidence that the children of trained parents had become better able to empathise with other people (Murray et al., 2016b; Vally, Murray, Tomlinson, & Cooper, 2015). Now this work is being extended to Lesotho mountain villages and other communities, including townships, in South Africa. Winnicott's legacy for our understanding of how the parent-baby relationship affects child development is immense. It is humbling to realise that, after all the decades of research that have followed his death, rather little about what we have found, if anything, would have surprised him. Rather, much of what we have learned broadly confirms his intuitions and clinical insight that what ordinary parents do, in ordinary ways and out of conscious awareness, is precisely what babies need. Nevertheless, as someone who likes to mine the empirical research evidence, I have found it has been intensely satisfying to see the detail and the substance revealed, and to feel that it can help us support parents caring for young babies.

Acknowledgements

I would like to thank the Winnicott Trust and John Davis for their support for the work conducted during my tenure of the Winnicott Fellowship. I would also like to pay tribute to the support I received from Martin James and from Madeleine Davis during this same period.

References

Cooper, P. J., Tomlinson, M., Swartz, L., Landman, M., Molteno, C., Stein, A. L., McPherson, K., & Murray, L. (2009). Improving quality of mother–infant relationship and infant attachment in socioeconomically deprived community in South Africa: randomised controlled trial. *British Medical Journal, 338*: b974.

Cooper, P. J., Tomlinson, M., Swartz, L., Woolgar, M., Murray, L., & Molteno, C. (1999). Post-partum depression and the mother–infant relationship in a South African peri-urban settlement. *British Journal of Psychiatry, 175*: 554–558.

Morrell, J., & Murray, L. (2003). Parenting and the development of conduct disorder and hyperactive symptoms in childhood: a prospective longitudinal study from 2 months to 8 years. *Journal of Child Psychology and Psychiatry, 44*: 489–508.

Murray, L., Arteche, A., Fearon, P., Halligan, S., Croudace, T., & Cooper, P. (2010). The effects of maternal postnatal depression and child sex on academic performance at age 16 years: a developmental approach. *Journal of Child Psychology and Psychiatry, 51*: 1150–1159.

Murray, L., Arteche, A., Fearon, P., Halligan, S., Goodyer, I., & Cooper, P. (2011). Maternal postnatal depression and the development of depression in offspring up to 16 years of age. *Journal of the American Academy of Child and Adolescent Psychiatry, 50*: 460–470.

Murray, L., Cooper, P. J., Arteche, A., Stein, A., & Tomlinson, M. (2016a). Randomized controlled trial of the effect of a home visiting intervention on infant cognitive development in peri-urban South Africa. *Developmental Medicine and Child Neurology, 58*(3): 270–276.

Murray, L., De Pascalis, L., Tomlinson, M., Vally, Z., Dadomo, H., MacLachlan, B., Woodward, C., & Cooper, P. J. (2016b). Randomized controlled trial of a book-sharing intervention in a deprived South African community: effects on carer-infant interactions, and their relation to infant cognitive and socio-emotional outcome *Journal of Child Psychology and Psychiatry*, in press.

Murray, L., Kempton, C., Woolgar, M., & Hooper, R. (1993). Depressed mothers' speech to their infants and its relation to infant gender and cognitive development. *Journal of Child Psychology and Psychiatry, 34*: 1083–1101.

Tomlinson, M., Cooper, P. J., & Murray, L. (2005). The mother–infant relationship and infant attachment in a South African peri-urban settlement. *Child Development, 76*: 1044–1054.

Vally, Z., Murray, L., Tomlinson, M., & Cooper, P. J. (2015). The impact of dialogic book sharing training on infant language and attention: a randomized controlled trial in a deprived South African community. *Journal of Child Psychology and Psychiatry, 56*(8): 865–873.

CHAPTER SIX

The irrepressible song

Kenneth Wright

> You speech, where speeches end …
> Oh, you transformation
> Of feelings into … audible landscape!
>
> Rilke: *On Music*

> These things that live on departure
> understand when you praise them: fleeting, they look for
> rescue through something in us, the most fleeting of all.
> Want us to change them entirely, within our invisible hearts,
> Into—oh, endlessly—into ourselves! Whosoever we are!
>
> Rilke: *Ninth Duino Elegy*

Introduction

Winnicott never developed a complete cultural theory but by mapping a path from primary creativity, through transitional phenomena and play, to art and religion (Winnicott, 1953, 1967a, 1967b, 1971), he suggested a way of thinking that others could develop in their own way (e.g., Kuhn, 2013). In this chapter, I am going to focus on a small part of this larger domain and discuss the role of *form* in artistic creation (Wright, 2009, 2013a, 2013b, 2013c, 2015). While "form" itself is not a Winnicottian term, the issue of form is always present in his thinking.

It has to be said that the concept of form in psychological discourse is often ambiguous because while it sometimes refers to the patterns *embedded in* experience and behaviour, at others it refers to patterns which have been *abstracted from* experience, symbolised in some way, and thereby made "visible". Transference illustrates this ambiguity, for while we can say that transference phenomena exist in the sense that they govern behaviour, they only become visible to contemplation through a kind of abstractive seeing (Szasz, 1963). Primary creativity and transitional phenomena are similar in this respect, for while both processes involve a relationship between concordant forms—between the "shape" of an infant anticipation and the "shape" of a maternal response, for example—such forms are embedded in ongoing transactions and lack conscious awareness.

If we accept that the forms of experience and interaction are rendered visible through a kind of abstractive seeing, we could suppose that this is the fundamental basis of creativity. We could then say that the primary creative act is one of *seeing* form in a previously undifferentiated whole and the act of *making*, of embodying the perceived form in a new structure, is actually secondary.[1] In other words, endowing things with form—perceiving the latent pattern in an experience—is itself an act of creation; it recreates the experience within a potentially symbolic domain, enabling it to be retrieved and held in consciousness. The American philosopher Susanne Langer argued that capturing experience in this way was a means of preserving it from transience and decay, and considered it to be a principal function of art:

> What makes a work [of art] important is not the category of its expressed feeling ... but the *articulation of the experiential form*. In actual felt activity the form is elusive, for it collapses into a condensed and foreshortened memory almost as fast as the experience passes; to hold and contemplate it requires an image which can be held for contemplation (1988, p. 29, italics mine).

Note how Langer puts this: *it requires an image* to hold experience in mind for contemplation. Images are better suited than words for capturing experience because they articulate and portray the experiential form.

It is worth remembering that although form creation underpins language and *may* lead to expression in words, it actually precedes words, developmentally and often creatively, and remains relatively independent of them. Moreover, its focus is not so much on pinpointing and naming the shared realities of the *objective* world as on capturing *subjective* states which are private and fleeting. From this perspective, the capture of lived experience within a form is a way of transforming it; it recreates and reinstates the fleeting moment on a symbolic level, making it both less ephemeral and more communicable. Form creation is like catching a butterfly; it enables one to hold the otherwise fleeting moment and say: "Look, this is what it was like!" Imaging experience does not name it but gives it a new life and a sort of immortality within the culture. The poet and critic Archibald MacLeish once wrote of the poet that his task was "to cage, to capture, the whole of experience, experience as a whole … in a meaningful form … or shape to which the emotions answer" (1960, pp. 16–17), and this, according to Langer, is the prime function of art.

The capture of meaningful patterns within a form requires that certain conditions be fulfilled. First, the form must be an accurate representation of the experience—it must be truthful. Second, it has to capture the essence of the experience—it is not like a photograph which records every detail but a form which abstracts those features which feel important or significant. Third, it must have the power to evoke the experience, to revive it in absentia, and morphological resemblance of form to experience is the key element in this regard. Non-verbal forms do not, like words, *refer to* experience—*they recreate its essential pattern.*

These criteria point to important similarities between art and psychoanalysis: both are concerned with capturing experience in order to "recollect it in tranquillity"; both are concerned with essences or basic structures rather than ephemera; and both are concerned with truth and representational integrity. Finally, both are concerned, albeit in different ways, with the resurrection of experience, and the self-enrichment to which this leads depends in large measure on the "truth" of the forms they create.

Aesthetic truth

In alluding to "truthful" creation, I am not of course referring to any kind of objective truth, only to a subjective experience of correspondence or "fit". One could think of this as an intuition of "truth", a sense that inside and outside are in that moment resonant or concordant. Both art and psychoanalysis are deeply concerned with truth in this sense, but since my focus here is artistic creation, I will illustrate what I mean by reference to art. I am going to quote from the French artist, Henri Matisse, who was deeply interested in his own artistic process and more than usually articulate about what he was doing. I should note that in the following quotations there is often ambiguity as to whether he is concerned with himself or his object, which follows from the fact that artist and object are virtually merged in the moment of creation. In the following remarks, Matisse underlines this sense of overlap between his created objects and himself:

> The work is the emanation, the projection of self. My drawings and canvasses are pieces of myself. Their totality constitutes Henri Matisse. I could also say that my canvasses are my real children.
>
> When the artist dies he is cut in two. There are lives of artists which are short. Raphael, Van Gogh, Gauguin, Seurat, for example. But these people expressed themselves completely. They died represented. And [so] they haven't finished living. (Interview with Andre Verdet, 1952)[2]

Given this almost Siamese twin sense of connection, it is not surprising to find that truth of expression, or representation, is a central issue. Thus Matisse says:

> I have within me something to express, through plastic means. I work as long as that has not come out ... At any rate, when one expresses a feeling [through one's art], it is nothing as long as one has not found its perfect form. (Interview with Leon Degand, 1945)

Note the phrase: *it is nothing as long as one has not found its perfect form*. The "perfect form", which he sometimes calls a "sign", is a very important concept for Matisse. A "perfect form" has the power to "encompass" an experience which is struggling for expression—"When you know an object thoroughly," he says, "you can encompass it with a contour that defines it entirely" (interview with Leon Degand, 1945). Encompassing the object in this way transforms its existential status; it captures the essence of the experience, brings it to life, and in this regard redeems it from nothingness. In this sense one could say that the artist creates *himself* through his work, redeems *himself* from nothingness. It is almost as though in a feeling sense, he does not fully exist—he is in a kind of limbo—until he can experience himself within his "perfect", created forms. We can begin to see why he feels that artists who have died young have not really died because "they died represented". To be "represented" within a form of your own creation is to be inscribed in the culture and insured against the depredations of time. The forms you have made are a means, and guarantee, of resurrection.

So how could we characterise these "perfect forms" which "encompass" the artist's experience? One thing is certain—they are not about appearances. They are not about capturing what a tree looks like, for example, but concern the artist's whole experience of the tree, and the way this gradually leads him to its essential nature. "The tree", says Matisse, "is the sum total of its effects on me. [I can only draw it] after *identifying* myself with it. I have to create an object that resembles [the *essence*, not the appearance of] the tree, and this essence can only be discovered through *identification*" ("Conversations with Louis Aragon: On Signs", 1942, italics mine). But note again the ambiguity. What is the essence which the artist is trying to capture? Is it the essence of the tree or the essence of his own being?

Statements such as these throw some light on the aesthetic process. The emergence of the "perfect form" follows a prolonged effort to identify with the object—something one could see as the artist's equivalent of primary maternal preoccupation (Winnicott, 1956)—and it captures an apprehension of the object which can only be obtained in this way. Authentic creation is a truthful capture of one's own experience; as Matisse says: "[The artist cannot use] the sign [perfect form] that other artists may have found for the tree … To reproduce that means reproducing something dead" ("Conversations with Louis Aragon: On Signs", 1942). A living created form has to arise from a deep identification with the object and from deep within oneself; if the artist fails to "penetrate" the tree, its essential form will elude him.

> Drawing [says Matisse] does not depend on forms being copied exactly as they are in nature or on the patient assembling of exact details, but on the profound feeling of the artist before the object that he has chosen, on which his attention is focused, and whose spirit he has penetrated … There exists an essential truth that must

be disengaged from the outward appearance of the objects to be represented. This is the only truth that matters. ("Exactitude Is Not the Truth", 1947, pp. 179–180)

It is interesting to compare this description of the creative process with that of the seventeenth century Japanese haiku poet, Matsuo Basho, as the two accounts show remarkable overlap. My source is *The Narrow Road to the Deep North* (Basho, 1966) a kind of travel diary in which "… readers will find … a random collection of what I have seen on the road, *views somehow remaining in my heart*—an isolated house in the mountains, or a lonely inn surrounded by a moor, for example" (ibid., p. 73). "[T]he views remaining in my heart" are clearly those that have touched the poet-traveller in significant ways—something that becomes clearer in his advice to would-be poets:

> Go to the pine if you want to learn about the pine or to the bamboo if you want to learn about the bamboo. [But] in doing so, you must leave your subjective preoccupation with yourself. Otherwise you impose yourself on the object and do not learn. (1966, p. 33)

We cannot be certain what Basho meant when he spoke of "your subjective preoccupation with yourself", but the statement seems to refer to all those things that might interfere with the poet's dedicated attention to the object and openness towards it. If we were talking about analysis, we might think about an analyst's preoccupation with theory, or technique, or making the right interpretations—all these things would get in the way of his openness to the patient and his capacity for identification. Basho continues:

> Your poetry issues of its own accord when you and the object have become one—when you have plunged deep enough into the object to see something like a glimmering there. However well-phrased your poetry might be, if your feeling is not natural—if the object and yourself are separate—then your poetry is not true poetry but subjective counterfeit (1966, p. 33)

Basho's advice to the poet and Matisse's advice to the artist are remarkably similar: second-hand forms (for example, theory-based interpretations) can never capture a living experience and produce true art (or true analysis). This can only be achieved through an utterly devoted identification; you have to "leave your subjective preoccupations behind", and plunge so deeply into the object that you are no longer separate from it. Out of this intense identification a "glimmering" appears—the presentiment of a form which illuminates both self and object in a moment of truth.

Art and self-discovery

The "truth" arising from such an identification is relational not factual. It does not reside in either the object or the subject, or even in the form itself, but depends on a newly constituted triangular relationship in which the form is a connecting bridge. The artist senses the glimmering truth of the connecting pattern; the emerging form embodies the pattern in a new creation. The recognition of the pattern is a kind of *eureka* moment: "I have found the form that I was looking for." And while from the artist's perspective this form is a truthful representation of the object's essence, it is in reality something "seen" in the object by the artist which offers him a truthful reflection of himself.

The poet Seamus Heaney once said that writing a poem was like an echo coming back to you; you create the form of your poem, thereby giving form to something in yourself, and you then experience yourself more fully within the form that you have made. The self has been inscribed in the form and is now echoed by it. Heaney notes, however, that sometimes this echo, or feeling of self-recognition, is mediated by forms that others have made. When you are taking your first steps as a poet, for example (or it could be your first steps as an analyst), you struggle to find your own voice. You don't yet know how to speak, who you are, what you want express or, indeed, how to express it. You are simply following the pull to write poetry (or to be an analyst) and you imitate and copy. Then one day,

> … you hear [something] coming back from somebody else, you hear something in another writer's sounds, that flows in through your ear, that enters the echo-chamber of your head, and delights your whole nervous system … This other writer has spoken something essential to you, something you recognise instinctively as a true sounding of aspects of yourself and your experience. (Heaney, 2002, p. 16)

Here too there is identification, a sense of Siamese twin connection; in the moment of connection, you and the other poet (or supervisor, or analyst or analytic writer), are one. You are no longer imitating or copying, using an external form; *his* voice, *his* form, is *your* voice, *your* form, and you make it your own in a deep and internally organised kind of way. Although Heaney is talking about the aspiring poet, he is also describing the quintessential experience of art (perhaps also of analysis when the analyst's words feel authentic and true). You feel that this poem, this piece of music, this painting or sculptural object has made a "true sounding" of something in *you*; it has "spoken" to *you*, and you feel yourself confirmed and recognised within its forms.

Aesthetic form

What, then, is it about forms of this kind that enables you to enter into them, inhabit them, and make them your own? By what means do they make such true soundings of your emotional depths? And why do they create a feeling of enhancement, of being more truly oneself within the aura of their influence?

I can't do justice to these questions in a short text but I want to suggest that Winnicott and Stern, with their concepts of mirroring and attunement, throw some light on what could be going on. However, before discussing their work I need to refer to Susanne Langer's understanding of the art object (1953, 1988). It is hard to summarise the work of this philosopher in a few lines, but she gave us the briefest definition of art I have ever seen: "Art", she wrote, "is the creation of forms symbolic of human feeling" (1953, p. 40). In other words, the art object is neither an *expression* of feeling, nor a *description* of it, but a certain kind of *symbolic* rendering of its form. In an always unique and individual way, art abstracts the shapes embedded in experience and reveals what they are like. It presents an *analogue* or *semblance* of feeling and experience in a form that in Langer's phrase "contain[s its] sense as a being contains its life" (1988, p. 38). Whereas language is *representational* and aims to *describe* experience, the forms of art are *presentational* and *portray* what it is like. Thus a musical phrase *presents* the "shape" of a feeling through its patterned musical progression, while a painting *portrays* the essence of an experience through its dynamic interplay of line, shape, and colour.

It follows from this that connecting with an art object is not a matter of understanding it in the way that we understand a statement or proposition. As Clive Bell (1914) appreciated, the feeling of connection with an art object is mediated directly through aesthetic forms. But whereas for him, the significance of these forms was *purely aesthetic*, a response to what he called their *inevitable sequences*, for Langer, their significance lay in their capacity to replicate and thus revive the forms of personal experience. In her view, the feeling of *inevitability* depends on the form being a *truthful* representation of emotion; when we sense that a form reflects our own experience, we extend our boundaries to include it and dwell within it.

This seems a suitable moment to bring in transitional objects and phenomena which in Winnicott's theory prefigure the world of cultural objects. We could say that the continuity he proposes between infant and adult experience depends on the fact that both sets of objects are able to revive experience and hold it in awareness. Just as the transitional object enables the baby to "hold" and recreate an experience of the mother's body, so the art object provides for the adult a holding and sustaining structure for core subjective states. If we further consider that the infant acquires the transitional object through a kind of creative discovery—by finding in the depths of the bit of blanket, the sensory *gestalt* of the mother's body—we can see how this finding resembles the creative process described by Matisse and Basho. We can imagine the baby too discovering a "sort of glimmering" in the bit of blanket and uttering a cry of "*Eureka*! I have found it."

But there the similarity ends, for while the baby was looking for, and found, the mother's *body*, Matisse and Basho were looking for, and found, an expressive *form*. In the first case, the gestalt of the mother's body remains embedded in concrete experience; in the second, it emerges as a signifier that the artist progressively refines (or makes more "truthful") as he seeks to capture an essence of experience in his carefully constructed creation. In this respect, the transitional object is only a rough and ready model for the art object with its complex expressive organisation, and I think that mirroring, with its later flowering in attunement, is a more appropriate starting point because its currency, the mother's facial expression, is from the beginning a discrete and disembodied form.

Art and self-attunement

In his groundbreaking paper on mirroring, Winnicott (1967a) asks the question: "What does the baby see when he or she looks at the mother's face?" And he answers that "What the baby sees is himself or herself (ibid., p. 112)." In other words, the mother's face is a mirror that reflects the infant's mood through the medium of her facial expressions, an account which implies that the baby, from an early stage, is able to relate to facial expressions as emotionally significant forms. The mirroring baby has moved beyond the concreteness of the transitional object to an appreciation of forms with emotional "meaning"; the mother's face is no longer a simple physical object—perhaps it never was—but is now a screen, with signifying expressions playing across it.

One could say more about Winnicott's theory, but because space is short, I am simply going to transpose his question into a different key, a different context, and ask: "What does the *artist* see when he (or she) looks at *the canvas he has painted*?" I want to suggest that the answer is in many ways similar to the one Winnicott gives in relation to mother and baby, namely that the artist sees himself.

This answer depends on the idea that the artist's creation is a *face-like* structure which generates for the viewer expressive forms which are not unlike facial expressions. In this model, the painting's "expressions" would be the forms within which the artist has captured the "essence" of his subject—in Matisse's case, the essence of the tree; in Cezanne's case, the essence of the mountain, and so on. But as before, we have to remember that creating these forms involved the artist *becoming* the tree, becoming the mountain, so the issuing forms are also reflections of his own sensibility.

Approaching artistic creation from this mirroring perspective invites one to see both process and artist in more dynamic terms. It reveals the artist as in need of mirroring forms, as engaged in a search for such forms as he interacts with the object world, and as striving to create them through his aesthetic work. It reveals him as trying to make good a maternal deficiency and as needing these forms to bring himself into being. It suggests that his work is a striving for self-recognition, not as Freud thought, by the public, but within the mirroring forms of his own creation. Driven by this need, the artist approaches himself and his medium in a state of aesthetic (primary maternal) preoccupation and struggles to sense what is going on in the depths. If fortune shines on him, a "glimmering" appears, and his task is then to cajole or coerce his medium to give form to that which he feels is there. In this account, the artist plays a dual role: in facing his medium as a source of forms he is like a child confronted with a less than responsive mother; as the one who creates the forms he is now a mother who moves heaven and earth to make a reflective connection with her child.

This view of the artist's creative process is enriched and elaborated by Stern's work on maternal attunement (1985). While in mirroring, the variety of responsive forms is limited by the expressive potential of the human face, in attunement such constraints are transcended and the mother mirrors her baby with face, voice, gesture, and movement in an irrepressible flowering of maternal forms. With this new variety of forms, she mirrors back to her baby every aspect of his experience which catches her attention; she now sings, dances, and enacts her baby into existence and says to him in a million different ways: "This is what you are like." *Pari passu*, we can see the baby as confronted with an endless theatre of forms—the mother is his poetry, his art, his drama, and his painting.

The attuning forms described by Stern are indeed similar in many ways to the forms of art as described by Langer: they are iconic and analogical, and they replicate the emotional contours of emotion, which Stern has termed the infant's "vitality affects" or "forms of vitality", and the mother would refer to as what her baby is feeling. The mother captures in her forms her "true soundings" of the infant; and as the expressive counterpart of her bodily adaptation in the feeding situation, they positively invite the infant to enter into them. Merleau-Ponty (1962, p. 146) once wrote that "I *live* in the facial expressions of the other"; and we might suppose, as Winnicott did, that the baby *lives*, and becomes more vibrantly himself, within the mother's responsive forms, just as we as adults become more alive and fully ourselves within the resonant forms of art.

From a theoretical perspective we could say that by putting her creative capacity at the infant's disposal, the mother offers the baby a rich and cumulative portrayal of what he is like. The forms she creates are her "presentational symbols" of his moment by moment experience, and she lays them out in the transitional space between them. They constitute an external phase of the infant self—a pool of accessible forms, or presentations, which in due course he may come to internalise. In the meantime, he can bask within their reflection, his sense of being and selfhood sustained within them. In a similar way we can think of the artist's creations as an external phase of his subjectivity, and by extension our own, a repository of self-created attunements which sustain his emotional being and keep it alive.

Art and psychoanalysis

In discussing the role of form in artistic creation I have made brief cross-references to psychoanalysis, and given time, I would have enlarged on the use of form and imagery in the consulting room. I have long thought that psychoanalysis and art have much in common, and this feeling was strengthened by my reading of Langer whose ideas meshed so well with those of Winnicott and Stern. Psychoanalysis also involves a symbolic recasting of experience and it wouldn't be hard to think of the analyst too as creator of life-giving forms, particularly when he stops interpreting. But if he is not interpreting, what *is* he doing? In our post-Winnicott, post-Bion era, we tend to talk of "holding" and "containing" as though their meaning was self-evident; Langer's theory of non-verbal symbolic forms provides an operational entry into what they could mean in practice. Her ideas invite us to think of imagery as the midwife of experience, and to reflect that until the patient *has* an experience—until it *exists* within a containing and resonating form—there is strictly speaking nothing to interpret.

Towards the end of his mirroring paper, Winnicott brings his reflecting metaphor into the heart of analytic work. It is, he says, not "clever and apt interpretations" which make the difference to the patient, but something more like the maternal facial expressions which "reflect what is there to be seen". He puts this whole idea in a beautiful and eloquent way, and it seems appropriate, on this occasion, to leave the last word to him (1971, p. 117):

> This glimpse of the baby's and child's seeing the self in the mother's face, and afterwards in a mirror, gives a way of looking at analysis and the psychotherapeutic task. Psychotherapy is not making clever and apt interpretations; by and large it is a long term giving back to the patient what the patient brings. *It is a complex derivative of the face that reflects what is there to be seen.* I like to think of my work this way, and to think that if I do this well enough, the patient will find his or her own self, and will be able to exist and to feel real. Feeling real is more than existing; it is finding a way to exist as oneself, and to have a self into which to retreat for relaxation. (Italics mine)

Notes

1. There is obviously more to creativity than abstracting forms from experience and reinstating them in new structures but in this paper, and following Winnicott, I am mainly concerned with the early development of creative capacity and how this might depend on maternal adaptation in the preverbal period. Winnicott saw that creativity was closely linked to symbolic development and the ability to transfer significant shapes and patterns from one object or context to another. In the absence of symbols there is no way that meaningful patterns can be grasped and held in the mind and no way of using them as psychic tools. As long as meaning is embedded in behaviour, it can only be reacted to unconsciously. In this paper, I focus on the stage when meaning is just beginning to detach itself from its embedded state and I look at some of the ways in which this emergence of meaning might be fostered.
2. All quotations from Matisse are from Flam, J. (1995).

References

Basho, M. (1966). *The Narrow Road to the Deep North and Other Travel Sketches*, N. Yuasi (Trans.). London: Penguin.
Bell, C. (1914). *Art*. Oxford: Oxford University Press.
Flam, J. (1995). *Matisse on Art*. Los Angeles, CA: University of California Press.
Heaney, S. (2002). *Finders Keepers*. London: Faber & Faber.
Kulm, A. (Ed.) (2013). *Little Madnesses. Winnicott, Transitional Phenomena and Clinical Experience*. London: Tauris.
Langer, S. (1953). *Feeling and Form*. London: Routledge & Kegan Paul.
Langer, S. (1988). *Mind: An Essay on Human Feeling*. Baltimore, MD: Johns Hopkins University Press.
MacLeish, A. (1960). *Poetry and Experience*. Peregrine Edition. London: Penguin.
Merleau-Ponty, M. (1962). *The Phenomenology of Perception*. C. Smith (Trans.). London: Routledge & Kegan Paul.
Stern, D. (1985). *The Interpersonal World of the Infant*. New York: Basic Books.
Szasz, T. (1963). The concept of transference. *International Journal of Psychoanalysis, 44*: 432–443.

Winnicott, D. W. (1953). Transitional objects and transitional phenomena—a study of the first not-me possession. *International Journal of Psychoanalysis*, *34*: 89–97; reprinted in *Collected Papers—Through Paediatrics to Psychoanalysis* (1958), London: Tavistock; and also in *Playing and Reality* (1971), London: Tavistock.

Winnicott, D. W. (1956). Primary maternal preoccupation. In: *Collected Papers—Through Paediatrics to Psychoanalysis* (pp. 300–305). London: Tavistock, 1958.

Winnicott, D. W. (1958). *Collected Papers—Through Paediatrics to Psychoanalysis*. London: Tavistock.

Winnicott, D. W. (1967a). Mirror role of mother and family in child development. In: *Playing and Reality* (pp. 111–118). London: Tavistock, 1971.

Winnicott, D. W. (1967b). The location of cultural experience. In: *Playing and Reality* (pp. 95–103). London: Tavistock, 1971.

Winnicott, D. W. (1971). *Playing and Reality*. London: Tavistock.

Wright, K. (2009). *Mirroring and Attunement. Self-Realisation in Psychoanalysis and Art*. Hove, UK: Routledge.

Wright, K. (2013a). Found objects and mirroring forms. In: A. Kuhn (Ed.), *Little Madnesses: Winnicott, Transitional Phenomena and Cultural Experience* (pp. 203–214). London: Tauris.

Wright, K. (2013b). The repressed maternal in Freud's topography of the mind. In: S. Akhtar & M. K. O'Neil (Eds.), *On Freud's "The Unconscious"* (pp. 160–178). London: Karnac.

Wright, K. (2013c). The search for form: A Winnicottian theory of artistic creation. In: J. Abram (Ed.), *Donald Winnicott Today* (pp. 250–269). Hove, UK: Routledge.

Wright, K. (2015). Maternal form in artistic creation. In: M. B. Spelman & F. Thomson-Salo (Eds.), *The Winnicott Tradition* (pp. 305–313). London: Karnac. Also in P. Townsend (Ed.), *Psychoanalysis and Artistic Process*. Free Association (special edition) (2014), *65*: 7–21.

CHAPTER SEVEN

Creativity in everyday life (or, Living in the world creatively)

Ken Robinson

I shall be drawing on Winnicott, using some of his ideas and even quoting him, but what I am about to write is not intended as an exegesis. I offer it simply as a statement of how I myself currently think about creativity in our everyday lives in the world.

Transitional phenomena

A colleague told me recently about a four-year-old preschool boy whom I shall call Jamie. Jamie was playing with his telescope. From the outside it was a stick. Jamie informed his teacher proudly that he could turn it into whatever he wanted it to be: "My telescope", he said, "could become anything." I don't think he had read Winnicott but in his simple and delightful way he catches the essence of play and creativity.

He doesn't say, "Look at my stick, it's like a telescope." For him the stick *is* a telescope, such is the seriousness of his engagement in play. At the same time—and this is Winnicott's paradox—the stick is a stick. His teacher is required to know this while not denying that it *is* a telescope. At another time the little boy might transform the stick-telescope into something else, perhaps a powerful drill so that instead of exploring the stars and the universe he can investigate the centre of the earth.

Here we have the child's (and later the adult's) capacity for creativity operating simultaneously with, and facilitated by, his sense of reality, and we have the importance of the environment in holding that sense of reality whilst also recognising the importance of play and creativity. It would be a mistake to assert shared reality and correct his equation of the stick with a telescope for he is quite capable of reality testing: he is not psychotic, though just as the dreamer enters a state of hallucinatory wishful psychosis so Jamie has "the ability to play about with psychosis" (Winnicott, 1965, p. 61) on the border of fantasy and reality. In contrast a patient of mine arrived one day in a terrible state. The milk carton that she was carrying with her in her briefcase for her coffee at work had split open and spilt into her case: it *was* semen and I *was* her abusive father who amongst other acts had forced fellatio onto her. She had lost the holding framework of reality and stood in need of careful help to disentangle fantasy and reality. This confused perceptual identity was not felt as creative by my patient but as persecutory, abusive, and traumatic: *delusion* had taken the place of *illusion*.

Of course, we could if we wish link the boy's use of his telescope with his particular phase of psychosexual development, as a display of potency to his female teacher, an oedipal play in which he seduces her just as he might playfully, but very seriously enjoy an affair with his mother, capturing her all for himself. But we should be careful, I think, not to concentrate solely on the content of this particular little boy's chosen illusion. To do so would be to miss the importance of a process—the creation of a creative illusion within the framework of shared reality that is held internally and externally, a process that is fundamental to health in our everyday lives.

It is in this way that we *find* ourselves every day in the world of objects around us and make that world our own. As Schopenhauer put it: "My representation is my world" (2008, I. 3). Creative living takes place in an area between two poles. On the one hand there is existing simply as an object in a world of objects, without imagination and without a sense of a living self—as one of my patients put it when she was emerging as a subject, existing in a state of being absent from one's own life. And on the other there is madness where reality does not have its due place, or to put it in the terms of John Locke (with whose work Winnicott was in implicit dialogue), where there is a failure to check on the conformity between one's fancies and reality. Locke accords imagination, as fiction, an important role in human life, but for him only so long as it does not obscure reality. Winnicott extended that role to make the capacity for illusion constitutive of the feeling of being alive and authentic in the context of an awareness, however tacit, of a shared reality, an awareness held first by the environment then internalised, with the environment in reserve should the internal need support. Something that exists objectively in the external world is given personal meaning by the subject: at the heart of personal meaning is a felt sense of being alive in relation to the world. Ontologically this personally experienced object has its being neither solely in the mind of the subject—that way lies solipsism, nor in the external objective world—that way lies dull and lifeless concretism—but in the intermediate realm between, in the third realm of transitional space.

An unfolding inherited potential for creativity: a developmental line

I'd like to highlight the role of reality as a *frame*, within which creative engagement can take place, and the internal and environmental holding of that frame. To do so I shall sketch in the path from the subjective object to the cultural field. You will be well acquainted with Winnicott's ideas about development so I shall be brief.

1. I start with the initial area of illusion between mother and baby as the environmental mother presents a piece of reality to the infant just as the infant has the illusion that he (or she) is creating it. This piece of reality is experienced as a subjective object. Reality is held by the environment and holding includes a sense of tact and timing as to when to introduce reality.
2. Reality continues to be held by the environment but there is a gradual development of a sense of reality, of a world out there which is not, or not wholly, under the control of the infant. It is here that tact and timing remain quintessentially important in titrating the dosage of reality that the infant must face. From another angle the infant must destroy the subjective object in order to experience it as an external object (and the object must survive). "In these ways the object develops its own autonomy and life, and … contributes-in to the subject, according to its own properties" (Winnicott, 1971, p. 106). The capacity to use a transitional object develops as part of the tactfully managed passage from an experientially narcissistic to an object-related world. The transitional object

is neither wholly inside nor wholly outside but, as Anna Freud pointed out, invested with both narcissistic and object libido, embodying properties of both the mother's and child's body (1965, p. 79).
3. Gradually the environmental holding of reality is internalised (along with other aspects of the environment that go to make up its internal representation) to provide a framework within which the object can be subjectively experienced, and the self experienced as alive without loss of a sense of shared reality. In the course of this development the continuing existence of the holding environment is essential.
4. Finally, the fate of the transitional object is to lose its meaning. As Winnicott puts it, "The transitional phenomena ... become diffused, ... spread out over the whole intermediate territory between 'inner psychic reality' and 'the external world as perceived by two persons in common', that is to say, over the whole cultural field. The transitional object may be 'relegated to limbo'" (1971, p. 6). But there is also a continuum as transitional phenomena within a shared reality remain as the fundamental ground on which creativity and aliveness rest.

The transitional object comes into being as a result of separation, but the third realm of transitional phenomena ensures that in one way separation is never total. Instead of the mother/environment/objective world existing in one world and the child and adult existing in another, " ... in health there is", as Winnicott puts it in a very condensed passage, "no separation, because in the space-time area between the child and the mother, the child (and so the adult) lives creatively, making use of the materials that are available—a piece of wood or a late Beethoven quartet" (1986, pp. 36–37). Elsewhere Winnicott comments: "The special feature of this place where play and cultural experience have a position is that *it depends for its existence on living experiences*, not on 'inherited tendencies'" (1971, p. 127, emphasis in the original).

An example of spontaneous living

With that word "depends" in mind I turn to a poem by William Carlos Williams, "The Red Wheelbarrow" (1987). I am using it not to talk about poetic creation but as capturing a simple act of apperception in which "so much depends upon" the slow meditative contemplation of the wheelbarrow (for a text of the poem, see https://www.poets.org/poetsorg/poem/red-wheelbarrow).

"The Red Wheelbarrow" is a reminder that creative apperception is not the sole province of poets and artists but an everyday achievement—Williams makes the point by preferring prosaic everyday language. The formal movement of his poem, which requires the reader to fill each word with and experience its meaning, catches the process of apperception as inseparable from the continuous process of becoming oneself, a process in which in principle each moment is a new unfolding of ourselves in the world. *That* is the meaning of the poem, *that* is what *depends on* a red wheelbarrow. As the onlooker's eye (and the reader's too) plays around the scene before him it pauses, breaks it down into parts (the red wheelbarrow, the rainwater that glazes it) and those parts into their parts (wheel/barrow; rain/water) in order to arrive at a new whole. I am reminded of Samuel Taylor Coleridge's account of imagination. In Coleridge's words, it " … dissolves, diffuses, dissipates, in order to recreate … It is essentially vital, even as all objects (as objects) are essentially fixed and dead." And, still in Coleridge's terms, in so doing it performs "a repetition in the finite mind of the eternal act of creation in the infinite I AM" (1817, p. 167). (I shall look later at the godlike implications of this statement.)

Destruction in the service of creativity

When Winnicott spoke of "inherited tendencies" he had in mind any inherited factor that works against the experience of being alive. I think that the phrase might be taken to include received consensual ways of seeing and responding to the world around us (and our own past ways of seeing and responding) that have to be challenged, *dismantled*, or *destroyed* in order to create and experience the world afresh in acts of personal apperception. Picasso recognised this when he famously said: "The urge to destroy is also a creative urge." Living personally in the world is not just a creative act, but a constant business of *dismantling, destroying, and recreating*, so as to refind the world as our own. In this sense history has to be undone to come alive in the present, though in coming alive our individual history of being alive will also be present. Even metaphor, itself a transitional phenomenon asserting not likeness or similarity but identity, dies through over-familiarity to become dead metaphor. Jamie's metaphoric stick-telescope will be discarded for the stick to take on new metaphoric vitality. Dead metaphor carries no personal meaning, but its meaning can be rediscovered.

The phenomenology of the actual experience of creating the world afresh is difficult to describe from the inside. The experience is tacit and instantaneous. But rather clumsily it goes something like this:

> I destroy the object that comes to me from the outside and it survives.
> I am in an alive receptive state, unintegrated.
> Now I can recreate the object for myself and it has its own properties that impact on me.
> The object is alive. I am alive in it and it in me (cf. Winnicott, 1971, pp. 105–106).

Here we have a reciprocal intercourse that has a precursor in the proto-conversations of infant and mother.

Although I am deliberately depicting apperception in a way that echoes the infant's experience I am not suggesting that it is regressive. I am saying that it contains within itself its own history in such a way that reiterated recreation is felt as continuous aliveness. And I am also saying, as Winnicott argued, that there is a continuum from the child's creation of the transitional object to mature creativity as the maternal environment gives way to the wider cultural environment. As Trevarthen and co-workers have shown, proto-conversations become improvisatory dialogues between jazz musicians (Schlögler & Trevarthen, 2007)—two examples are the musical conversations of Keith Jarrett and Charlie Haden or Andy Sheppard and Rita Martoculli.

Discovering ourselves in the world and the world in ourselves

Each encounter with the objective world is a fresh invitation to find ourselves in it *and also it in ourselves*, transcending the boundaries between self and other. Another poem by Williams (entitled simply "POEM") will clarify what I have in mind (for a text of the poem see http://www.poemhunter.com/poem/poem-as-the-cat/). In this poem the suspension of syntax between lines and stanzas represents the subject's kinaesthetic internalisation of a cat's carefully poised movement as it climbs over the jam cupboard into a flowerpot. Williams offers no hidden or symbolic meaning; instead to perform his poem is to enact a harmony of subject and object. While the cat moves the reader moves and merges with it, internalising its movements, becoming the cat in a very particular act of meaning.

That is, it is not simply, as the Romantic model would have it, that we shed light on a world that would otherwise remain dead, but that our interaction with objects sheds light on us, alters us. We are in dialogue with our worlds. We recognise (re-cognise) ourselves in the objects that we create in an echo of the way that the infant finds himself in the mirror of the mother's face. Such an exchange extends our sympathetic boundaries and challenges rather than simply adds to what we think we might already know about both the world and ourselves. This is something that T. S. Eliot understood in relation to poetry: the truly new work of art alters the existing order "if ever so slightly" and requires readjustment of each work towards the whole body of poems, old and new (1953, p. 23). So Williams's poems record what it is like not just to register that there's a red wheelbarrow or cat and a flowerpot and so on but to attend to a unique scene without preconception. Each new encounter with the world, like each new work of art, demands that we meet it afresh without imposing expectations. We must be prepared to allow it to alter us and revise what we already know. (I am aware that I could well be referring here to the process of analytic listening.)

Experiencing with the bodily self

Williams's "POEM" serves as a reminder that the act of creative apperception (I AM) relies on body experiences. It brings together subject and outside world in vital interrelation through the medium of a bodily self, through indwelling in the body, an awareness of being alive in a body. Williams had a dictum: "no ideas but in things". The equivalent here might be: "no self but in body". It is with this bodily self that we can, in a particular form of transitional space, know the object by being it, by empathically recreating its bodily state within our bodily selves through imitation, through *Einfühlung*. Rooted in Freud's thinking, itself inspired by Theodor Lipps, this notion of knowing through imitative empathic engagement has a long history in psychoanalysis—there is currently a resurgence of interest in embodied empathy fuelled partly by the discovery of mirror neurons—but in talking about the bodily self in this way we are not simply in the realm of psychoanalytic hypothesis. This is a form of knowing that crosses historical and cultural boundaries. For example, the Japanese poet Doho, following his master Basho, taught that in order to write about an object the poet must "enter into the object, sharing its delicate life and feelings" (Basho, 1985, p. 14). And in much the same way the Kalahari Bushmen imitate the animals that they hunt:

> When you track an animal you must become the animal. You feel a tingling in your armpits when the animal is close .... When the springbok heart beats in your ribs, you see through its eyes. You feel its drive, dark on your cheek. (Foster & Foster, 2000)

Varieties of creative apperception

There is a danger that I might seem to be saying that creative living in the world consists of a series of godlike moments, when, as Milner put it, "... the original 'poet' in each of us creates the outside world for us," moments "that are too much like visitations of the gods to be mixed with everyday thinking" (Milner, 1987, p. 88). On the contrary. Williams's poems are celebrations of acts of apperception that we all know without attending to them as poets. We take them for granted unless we lose them. The feeling of being alive and spontaneous, of I AM, belongs to experiences as various as shopping in the local supermarket, cooking, eating at a favourite restaurant, taking a photograph, playing the saxophone badly, listening to John Coltrane, enjoying an evening at the theatre, meeting a new acquaintance, being with a loved one, or the epiphanic experiences that Milner found expressed in the work of Thomas Traherne. There are, however, different registers to such experiences: some happen in the background, some in the foreground, as, for example, the godlike moments that Milner writes about (to Winnicott's approval [Winnicott, 1971, pp. 44–45]). We can live without them for a time, as an infant without the ministrations of his mother, but if they do not return after a bearable period the discontinuity in the experience of being alive may be traumatic. At worst, we might be left feeling like Macbeth, that in place of aliveness is a void, that "Life ... is a tale/Told by an idiot, full of sound and fury/Signifying nothing" (Shakespeare, 1623, V. v. 26–28). Nothing *depends* on such a void.

A sense of reality as a frame: the gallery and the theatre

I return now to the importance of a sense of reality as a frame for creative engagement. In a painting the frame literally marks out the area of illusion within it, as if to say this is the solid frame (reality), and that (the painting) is illusion. The painter and printmaker Howard Hodgkin subverts such a rigid distinction, his expression of a particular moment or experience spilling out spontaneously beyond the confines of the frame onto the frame itself.

Take, for example, his painting "Wet Evening" where he superimposes an irregular painted frame on the regular wooden one with hints of a recession of further frames (for a full colour copy of the painting see https://howard-hodgkin.com/artwork/wet-evening). His painting destroys the received static frame. Its spontaneous, free-flowing brushstrokes bursting with vibrant colour create their own more appropriate personal frame that scarcely contains them. The painting's ecstatic celebration of light, colour, movement, and sexuality invites us into its inner depth, thrusts out towards us, and pushes against the boundaries of the frame. But this transitional frame remains nevertheless a frame which in the gallery is further framed by the wall on which it hangs so that its fluid boundaries are paradoxically sharply delineated. William Blake thought of the line that he drew around his figures as a "bounding line", an alive leaping boundary (Blake, 1809, XV, K585). Hodgkin's frames are "bounding" frames, but frames for all that. The frame provides the security within which the viewer can enter into the painting and let it enter into him.

A sense of reality as a frame is equally important for creative apperception in the context of the everyday experience of going to the theatre or cinema. Winnicott acknowledged that he had "derived most of [his] concepts from those of Freud" (1986, p. 21). Perhaps in terms of the concept of play he found Freud's "Psychopathic Characters on the Stage" (1942a) helpful for its account of the nature of the intermediate realm between play and reality in the theatre. Freud had written that "being present as an interested spectator at a spectacle or play does for adults what play does for children, whose hesitant hopes of being able to do what grown-up people do are in that way gratified". They too understand through being the object, through identifying themselves with the hero. Freud goes on: "[The spectator's] enjoyment is based on an illusion; that is to say, his suffering is mitigated by the certainty that, firstly, it is someone other than himself who is acting and sufferingfon the stage, and, secondly, that after all it is only a game, which can threaten no damage to his personal security" (pp. 305–306).

Adults in the theatre play seriously at being Oedipus or Hamlet in the knowledge that they are watching a play. Where the early environment held reality for the child so that he or she could play in its presence, in the theatre reality is held by its being a theatre, with programmes, seats, proscenium arch (if there is one), intervals, and so on. It is also held by our inner sense of the formal structure of the play which John Yorke has recently argued has deep roots in our psyches. Our knowledge that we are watching a five act or a three act play provides a frame within which we are free to empathically enter the drama before us. The tacit knowledge that we are in a shaped story (unlike the messy reality that we enter from and return to) holds us as we lose ourselves in the drama as if real. As Yorke puts it, structure and form embody "every tale['s] … attempt to lasso a terrifying reality, tame it and bring it to heel" (2014, p. 217). All writers and directors worth their salt will run their own variations on this structure but when it is put under great pressure (even to breaking point), when the frame is threatened, empathic play can become precarious and cease. Such is the case in *King Lear* for example, where it can feel that terrifying reality has not been tamed and brought to heel. The tragic possibility that Lear is mad and delusional as he holds the dead Cordelia in his arms can feel unbearable and render us unable to sustain our sense of being in a state of play. Dr Johnson did not speak for his age alone when he found *King Lear* too painful to read, though few would, I think, prefer Nahum Tate's feel-good version. Or to take another example, Lucy Bailey's 2014 production of *Titus Andronicus* was so realistically harrowing that members of the audience fainted and vomited. For them reality broke through and shattered their play-state in much the same way that we awaken from a dream-state when the dream becomes too much to process. The fact of this being a drama was held neither externally by the theatre and production nor internally. Winnicott was right in thinking of play as non-orgastic.

Play in the consulting room

Although I am concentrating on everyday creativity perhaps I can be allowed a footnote on play in the everyday work in the consulting room, on "the transference as a playground", a phrase taken from Freud's "Remembering, Repeating and Working-Through" (1914g, p. 154). As you know, Freud saw transference in this playground as an "intermediate region between illness and real life" and the analyst's task as allowing it "to expand in almost complete freedom" (p. 154), so that with the analyst's help it could be given a new meaning, remembering replacing repetition. Others have thought of the playground as a theatre in which the patient enacts and casts the analyst in transference roles which it is best for him not to enact but in which he has thoughts and feelings appropriate to his role. Whether we think of transference as playground or theatre, what starts out unbeknown to the patient as compulsive repetition of the past can become collaborative reflection, facilitated by the analyst's capacity to provide the conditions under which repetition is transformed into play. This capacity includes holding the reality that the intermediate realm of transference play is an "as if" realm, a realm of illusion (especially when it is lost or in danger of being lost by the patient). It also includes intuitive tact and timing in bringing the transference within the reach of the patient. Here too in this playground there is the possibility of a special form of personal knowledge.

Conclusion

When we enter into the dialogue between our inner world and the external world (which speaks back "according to its own properties") we open up the deeper reaches of our personalities. I have concentrated on the process rather than the content of such creative interaction. By way of conclusion I would like to emphasise that Jamie's telescope is a reminder that Winnicott the analyst also made a significant contribution to our understanding of personal knowledge. In the idea of the transitional object we have the core of what it means to live one's life creatively in the world. Writers and thinkers from Plato in the *Meno* to Michael Polanyi with his analysis of the tacit dimension of personal knowledge, to the literary critic F. R. Leavis who also formulated a concept of a third realm of knowledge, to Winnicott's brother-in-law, the philosopher Karl Britton, have wrestled with how to conceptualise "personal knowledge" (Britton, 1969; Leavis, 1975; Polanyi, 1958). The relation of Winnicott's to Britton's work is a study yet to be written. Where Winnicott asked, "What makes life worth living?" Britton was concerned with what contribution philosophy could make to the question of "What is the meaning of life?" and in his later years Britton became interested like Winnicott in a form of knowing which is neither rationalist nor empiricist. Like Winnicott he was also interested in a third area of knowledge. Britton thought that when we experience moments of intense personal knowledge we neither know anything empirical about the world nor do we have to regard them as simply evidence of mental states (though they can be so regarded). "They are taken, each one, as 'something understood'—neither explaining nor explained, but understood" 1984, p. 51). Winnicott brought psychoanalytic understanding to bear on the problem of "personal knowledge" and gave it its place in his theory of the development of the self experienced as alive through play, "the basis of ... the whole of man's experiential existence" (1971, p. 75). His contribution was to give a non-dualistic account of how in everyday life we develop the capacity to experience the world as subjectively real whilst accepting consensual reality, to create reality for ourselves whilst accepting objective reality.

References

Basho, M. (1985). *On Love and Barley: Haiku of Basho*. L. Stryk (Trans.). London: Penguin.
Blake, W. (1809). *A Descriptive Catalogue of Pictures*. London: J. Blake.
Britton, K. (1969). *Philosophy and the Meaning of Life*. Cambridge: Cambridge University Press.
Britton, K. (1984). Wonders. In: I. Dilman (Ed.), *Philosophy and Life: Essays on John Wisdom* (pp. 49–60). The Hague: Martinis Nijhoff (International Philosophy Series, vol. 17).
Coleridge, S. T. (1817). *Biographia Literaria: or, Biographical Sketches of My Literary Life and Opinions*. London: Dent, 1965.
Eliot, T. S. (1953). *Selected Prose*. London: Penguin.
Foster, C., & Foster, D. (2000). *The Great Dance: A Hunter's Story*. Cape Town: Earthrise Productions.
Freud, A. (1965). *Normality and Pathology in Childhood*. London: Hogarth.
Freud, S. (1914g). Remembering, repeating and working-through (further recommendations on the technique of psycho-analysis, II). *S. E., 12*: 145–156. London: Hogarth.
Freud, S. (1942a). Psychopathic characters on the stage. *S. E., 7*: 303–310. London: Hogarth.
Leavis, F. R. (1975). *The Living Principle. "English" as a Discipline of Thought*. London: Chatto & Windus.
Milner, M. (1987). *The Suppressed Madness of Sane Men*. London: Tavistock.
Polanyi, M. (1958). *Personal Knowledge*. London: Routledge & Kegan Paul.
Schlögler, B., & Trevarthen, C. (2007). To sing and dance together: from infants to jazz. In: S. Bräten (Ed.), *On Being Moved. From Mirror Neurons to Empathy* (pp. 281–302). Amsterdam, The Netherlands: John Benjamins.

Schopenhauer, A. (2008). *The World as Will and Presentation*. R. E. Aquila (Trans., in collaboration with D. Carus). New York: Longman.
Shakespeare, W. (1623). *Macbeth*. Third Series (The Arden Shakespeare). S. A. Clark & P. Mason (Eds.). London: Bloomsbury, 2014.
Williams, W. C. (1987). *The Collected Poems of William Carlos Williams, Vol. I: 1909–39*. A. W. Litz & C. MacGowan (Eds.). Manchester, UK: Carcanet. See also https://www.poets.org/poetsorg/poem/red-wheelbarrow.
Winnicott, D. W. (1965). *Maturational Processes and the Facilitating Environment: Studies in the Theory of Emotional Development*. London: Hogarth.
Winnicott, D. W. (1971). *Playing and Reality*. London: Penguin.
Winnicott, D. W. (1986). *Home Is Where We Start From*. London: Penguin.
Yorke, J. (2014). *Into the Woods. A Five Act Journey into Story*. London: Penguin.

CHAPTER EIGHT

Images and words: some contemporary perspectives on the concept of regression

Angela Joyce

It is a timely moment to revisit the concept of regression, which has had a central role in psychoanalytic theories of development, mental functioning, and clinical practice. Despite questions as to its usefulness and relevance in contemporary psychoanalysis, it remains, accruing controversy and disturbing or challenging us. I will revisit some of these controversies but here I want to think about some of the implications of the work of some contemporary French psychoanalytic thinking concerning so-called topographical regression and how it connects with Winnicott and work within the Independent tradition here in the UK. That is, regression from the so called "word" to the "thing" presentation in Freud's account.

The concept of regression arose in two overlapping domains, metapsychology and clinical practice as Freud (and others) sought to develop the conceptual and theoretical frame of psychoanalysis, and practising analysts (the same people!) engaged in the challenges of the clinic. The idea of the return to a former or less developed state has proved a useful tool in many ways and I think continues to be so in our quest to understand our patients.

Critics of the various applications of the concept (topographical, temporal, and formal regressions), have focused largely on clinical aspects of work with non-neurotic patients. The substance of Ferenczi's disputes with Freud in the 1920s and '30s concerned these patients, and led to what Michael Balint described as "a trauma on the psychoanalytic world" (1968, p. 152). Although it is Winnicott who is often regarded as the analyst who brought to attention the idea of regression to dependence, it was Ferenczi who promoted the idea of the analyst behaving "rather like an affectionate mother who will not go to bed at night until she has talked over with the child all his current troubles ..." (1931, p. 477). He was especially interested in how classical technique might retraumatise particular patients, and he picked out the "analyst's cool expectant silence and his failure to manifest any reaction" as risking the repetition of what he saw as the original trauma situation with the parents in childhood.

Ferenczi's ideas, however, did not go away and Michael Balint especially expanded his analyst's examination of these challenges in the consulting room (1968). Here the idea of therapeutic regression emerged, typically associated with the patient's dependence upon the analyst. Some writers have criticised it as somehow serving the needs of the analyst rather than the patient, and the various experimental changes to the setting came in for much condemnation. Responding to, staying in the area of the regression instead of something seemingly "hotter", manifest currently in the relationship between the analyst and patient, has often been viewed with suspicion and has gone along with the hegemony of the focus on the so-called "here and now" of the session.

Winnicott's writings about regression (1954a, 1954b) are to be included here as he also experimented with technique in order to deal with clinical challenges, and like Ferenczi observed the possible contribution of the analyst to patients getting stuck in their analyses. The kinds of patients he was describing were those who were most likely to have suffered impingements in their early life interfering with the establishment of the true self; to have not become "whole persons", and who function at the level before the "space-time unit status" has been achieved. For DWW it became fundamental for the analyst to facilitate the patient establishing his (or her of course) true self if that had been lacking, and of the patient getting to the position where *he* could speak his experience. This was far more important, as he wrote, than the analyst making clever interpretations.

Those aspects of the clinical implications of our various concepts of regression remain live issues, and in any discussion we may want to return to them. But now I want to turn to a very particular aspect, focused on Freud's ideas about mental functioning, and the creation of the dream and symptoms (1900a).

The concept of topographical regression was developed by him in his search to understand the mind, its functioning, and the process of dreaming and symptom formation. Under the influence of sleep, the dreamer is prevented from putting thoughts into action and instead produces dream images, pictorial presentations. This production of images is thought of as a "regression", with the implication that words, and even motoric actions were "progress". This linear model polarises the imagistic, pictorial, and perhaps even the affective quality of primary process, away from rational, conscious, secondary processes. There are many ways in which this can be discussed but in the space I have I want to explore one aspect, and that is to think about this polarity and whether it helps us in our work.

Here I will draw on a significant figure from the Independent tradition, Charles Rycroft (1981). He mounted a *hefty* criticism of Freud's theory of the dream process, especially the idea of topographical regression. Rycroft recast dream theory and primary process in his appeal to the integration of imagination not as rooted in pathological processes as he saw it, but drawing on human creativity. He eschewed what he saw as Freud's pathologising of "the non-verbal, iconic mode as irrational, characteristic of dreamers, neurotics, lunatics, infants and primitive peoples" and especially the idea that the capacity to use secondary process is dependent on the repression of primary process. Instead if one starts from the assumption that primary and secondary processes coexist from the beginning and continue to function in harmony in healthy development, one providing the imaginative and the other a rational basis for living, then we have a different psychoanalytic model of mental functioning, and perhaps a different way of thinking about some aspects of the analytic process.

Although Rycroft doesn't reference Winnicott's (1949) paper "Mind and Its Relation to Psyche—Soma", his model is very close to that proposed in it. The psyche, most closely linked to the soma, is there described as the "imaginative elaboration of somatic parts, feelings and functions, that is of physical existence". Early in development as the baby becomes a going concern, this psychosomatic unity is felt by "the individual to form the core of the imaginative self". This is dependent upon the mother's capacity to imaginatively elaborate her baby in her holding care. Mind, the capacity for thought, arises then in the context of what he calls "negative care", or "alive neglect", the opportunity the mother affords her baby as she introduces the "world in small doses", and is integrated into the *unit status* of the child. If this process is not managed by the holding mother's care, then potential disaster ensues. And this is what I want to focus upon: the impact of early relational trauma on the *unit status* of the child. What are the consequences when the child's soma/psyche/mind fail to achieve integration and unity? Especially what are the consequences for the integration of the child's sense of his bodily self, his imagination, his emotions, and his capacity to symbolise, play, speak, and talk.

Now a vignette from the work of one of my supervisees

Her patient was almost five years old when he entered intensive therapy, developmentally delayed by about twelve to eighteen months including severe language delay, emotionally volatile, and particularly jealous towards his younger half-sister. He had little symbolic play and his tantrums included biting and screaming. He had been removed from his birth mother because of severe neglect when he was nine months old and following a two-year period of foster care he was placed with his adoptive parents.

Some brief extracts from that work[1]

Aaron's play was repetitive and sensorimotor in nature, with little sense that his actions held symbolic meaning for him:

> He took the nesting egg and rolled it with intent. It smashed and the shells separated as they rolled about the room. He crawled after them, tapping them across the room ... He took the stacking cups and rolled them to me and I rolled them back one by one and sometimes two at a time together. I demonstrated the distinction of "together" and "apart". He copied this, but although he was able to say "together", he never said "apart".
>
> In a session not long after this one Aaron developed a game with the nesting egg rolling along the table until it reached the edge, at which point he would catch the egg just in time, before it fell to the ground and into pieces. Sometimes he did not catch it and his body would jerk spasmodically as it smashed, indicating his somatic, sensory registering of the smash.

> Watching the digger and the dumper truck from my window, picking up dirt and dumping it onto a lorry, he took a spellbinding interest. Together, we imitated with our arms the actions of the machine lifting, turning, and then dropping. Aaron whispered the word "drop" as if it carried great meaning for him. I began to explore with him what it might feel like to be dropped like the mud held together in the grip of the dumper, or the egg—with all the shell pieces scattered everywhere. I said that someone needed to help put these pieces back together; I was here to help him with all of his scattered feelings; together we could pick up the pieces and try to make sense of them, and work towards making him feel whole again. I allowed myself to be more playful: I sang, danced, and provided full yet brief sentences to describe what was happening around us whilst also describing his feelings as I sensed them.
>
> Soon he asked me, "More talking please." He wanted me to help him create a story: "More talking, more talking Coretta!"

Through this three times per week analytic therapy Aaron made great strides in recovering from the traumas of his young life, evident in his capacities and pleasure in talking, playing, as well as his attachments to the important people in his life. Much later as they were preparing for the end of therapy there seemed to be some regression in these capacities. His therapist noted how nervous he seemed and in contrast to how he usually was, he struggled to move a chair and didn't ask for her help.

> I commented on him being frightened to ask. He clowned around and poked his tongue out, seemingly in order to avoid the anxiety he felt. I persisted however, and then he said in a loud, clear voice, "My words are broken." He looked vulnerable and desperate. Together we managed to work out that somehow he couldn't phrase the question he needed to ask for help with the chair. I said that he was telling me that he needed my words to help him fix his broken words and that is what we have been doing in therapy.

This little boy's words, his broken, eloquent words, spoke volumes about how his therapy had mended his early broken self and how that remained as a marker in his being, now re-presenting itself as he approached another major loss but one which could now be articulated and mourned rather than suffered defencelessly and traumatically. Later in this chapter I will be thinking about how the child or adult patient "reaching for something" as DWW said, might be understood in broad terms within the ideas about regression.

This example gives us an opportunity to observe not only a very talented psychotherapist in action, but also the consequences for a young child of severe early relational trauma on his development. His lack of language as well as the paucity of his other symbolic functions is notable. His therapist's responses across the domains of soma, psyche, and mind bring to our attention the way we might use the whole of our capacities in this challenging work.

I am thinking about my own experience, especially with children who don't do what the books tell them to do in therapy, but "act out" instead; how difficult it is just to speak, never mind give finely honed interpretations! These children use their bodies to convey what their minds cannot—they can be very aggressive—shouting, hitting, biting, intruding into the body of the therapist, running in and out of the room, etc., etc.; words can often be experienced and used as weapons; they are felt to be inflammatory and provoke explosions rather than create connections. Or the opposite, when there is a crippling inhibition at work, and retreat and withdrawal seems the safest option. It is a real challenge often to find ways of being in the room with such children, and adults who are in similar states of mind. Many of these patients aren't in states of regression: they have never developed sufficiently to achieve a regression! In Anna Freud's language they have suffered developmental arrest. In Winnicott's they have never had sufficient of a facilitating environment to establish a true self, become a "whole person". Winnicott was also clear that in order to help such patients in analysis there had to have been sufficient construction of a self: a false self, an organised defence against the trauma of impingement, to engage in the analytic cure. In "Residential Care as Therapy" (1970) DWW said: "Even in a suitable case for classical psychoanalysis the *main thing* is the provision of conditions in which this kind of work can be done and in which the patient's unconscious cooperation can be gained to produce material for verbalisation" (p. 224, my italics). For these patients, children or adults for whom a sense of aliveness and feeling real has not been established, it is the setting: the analyst's reliable, holding presence that is the most significant therapeutic factor rather than the creation of insight through verbalised interpretation. This "reliable, holding presence" pertains to properties of the analyst's psyche/soma and mind, closely linked with the idea of the analyst as a maternal figure. This is not a simplistic or sentimental idea; rather it captures a complex making available to the patient the analyst's capacities, carefully honed in the transference–countertransference field, to the needs of the patient. And it includes the analyst's capacity to be affectively alive, including the capacity for hate. Easier said than done often, as the challenges are enormous!

There is an increasing contemporary interest in the consequences of early trauma which, within psychoanalysis, has come to be conceptualised as the area of non-represented states of mind, where there are holes, so to speak, in the fabric of the psyche; rents in the warp and weft of that fabric where experience has not even reached the state of representation, and sensory, somatic sensation predominates. What does this look like in the consulting room? We can see it in the case of Aaron in his persistent rolling and smashing of eggs.

To take another example from a supervisee[2]

> Her child patient had an early life suffused with impingement from a mentally ill mother, loss through continuous changes of foster placements, and eventually adoption at the age of rising six years old. After two years of complex intensive psychotherapeutic work, through which this girl, Lottie, was establishing a more alive, real sense of herself, the possibility of her being able to contemplate missing her therapist during a break seemed very far away. We might postulate the necessary defences she would have to hold onto in order to survive this implied loss, but we wondered together whether this child had just not ever been able to conceive of the experience of "missing", at an emotional level, never given it representation. She had come to know the idea and could see that she was missed, but it seemed that indeed there was a hole in her psyche where for her, there might have been a sense of missing, longing, yearning. The work of her therapy still requires something that can help her represent, know at an emotional level that she misses, has lost someone who means something to her.

Interest in this area has been particularly strong in the French psychoanalytic tradition and has reached the UK via the translated works of Andre Green and Sara and Caesar Botella amongst others. These writers also stress the challenges to the analyst, and bring another way in which the metaphor of analyst as maternal presence can be thought about.

Andre Green is renowned for drawing our psychoanalytic attention to "absence". His best-known paper translated into English, "The Dead Mother" (1980) describes the sudden and radical absence of the maternal mind in the context of her seemingly alive presence—profound decathexis. The "dead mother complex" results, a place of the void, blank mourning, absence. The negative hallucination, or the framing structure, of the psychically dead mother creates a space in the child's mind which cannot be filled with fantasy, affects, imaginings, but with psychic holes, voids refilled by expressions of destructiveness freed by the weakening of the affectionate bonds, and secondary to the central loss of the mother's investment in her baby.

In terms of the challenge to the analyst, eschewing the classical approach Green says that he prefers to use: "… the setting as a transitional space, making an ever-living object of the analyst, who is interested, awakened by his analysand, giving proof of his vitality by the associative links he communicates to him, without ever leaving his neutrality" (p. 163).

In other words, Green proposes that the analyst conducts himself with these kinds of patients in an alive way, giving the patient the experience of his emotional investment, accessing his own imaginative capacity through his attention to his preconscious and particularly bearing in mind the risk that the patient feels intruded upon. This is necessary so as not to recreate, repeat, and reinforce the dead mother complex. This would be especially likely through excessive silence or the focus of interpretation of the patient's destructiveness as primary. Monica Lanyado has written in her book *The Presence of the Therapist* (2004) specifically about the demands made on the therapist to be an alive presence when working with children who have suffered catastrophic trauma. Anne Alvarez writes in her books *Live Company* (1992) and *The Thinking Heart* (2012) of providing the neglected or traumatised child with an experience where the therapist believes in "a brighter future than that which the self could conceive" (2012, p. 151).

Caesar and Sara Botella, coming out of the same French psychoanalytic milieu, go further in their explorations of what goes on in the analyst's mind when finding themselves in this territory. In their extended study of what they call "the work of psychic figurability" (2005) they propose that the analyst needs to be in a particular state of regression, or "regredience" (their translation of Freud's German *"regrediente"*, topographical regression), in order to respond to trauma that has rent the mind of the patient. They say this translation evokes something more transformational than "regression", with its possible pathological connotations. It is associated with a specific capacity of the dream work which, according to Freud, has preserved intact a primary quality of psychic functioning, that of recasting an idea into sensory images; the regredience of the word presentation to the thing presentation, or topographical regression. As they define "regredience" it *"is a psychic field, at once a state, a quality and movement in a process of evolution, a potential for transformation, a permanent psychic capacity for transforming in an endo-hallucinatory manner, any quality of excitation, verbal, motor or emotional"* (C. Botella, 2013, p. 104, emphasis in the original). In other words they are interested in what the analyst's mind produces, in the evocation of the visual image, about which Freud wrote in relation to dreams, especially through the use of metaphor. They propose the analyst draws upon this capacity in order to reach and give form to those unrepresented states in particular patients.

> They give an example of a four-year-old boy, Thomas, who had suffered multiple surgeries in his first twenty months. He had some seemingly autistic features but sought relationships which he couldn't then sustain. He was preoccupied with sensory experiences and particularly sound. He would make "Grrr ..." noises and at the end of sessions would become very distressed, not able to respond to the analyst's interpretations of the meaning of the separation. The analyst, faced with this terrified child then "had a nightmare". At this point he said to Thomas: "Grrr .... Grrr! You are afraid of the wolf!" accompanied by imitations of biting and clawing of the wolf. Although Thomas was terror stricken he calmed and was able to leave and subsequently was able to use this "Grrr. Grrr ... the wolf", to manage the transition and loss at the end of his sessions. What they describe here is the capacity of the analyst to use this process of regredience to double up with Thomas, be in the same state as him, his nightmare, and then give voice to his terror. The image, furnished by the analyst, like that in the dream work, linked to the possibility of representation in memory, which they suggest enables the past to become memory rather than remain as a psychic hole.

Bollas, Wright, and recently Michael Parsons, amongst others, have written about the analytic setting providing a space for the evocation of idioms of the self, not specifically with patients who have suffered early trauma, but as a most important function of the analytic relationship. Winnicott's squiggle technique uses this "regredient" capacity and we can see in many of his accounts how the image constitutes his interpretation to the child of his predicament. It seems clear that this capacity has its origins in the earliest infant-mother relationship, which when good-enough, is rich with the imaginative elaboration of sensory experiences, the stuff of archaic representation. The idea that it requires a regression, or regredience in the analyst is an interesting question. How far do we go along with Rycroft's critique of Freud, in claiming that in health these are integrated capacities and available then to the analyst in her free floating attention to give form to the patient's unconscious states?

I want here to explore this link between the work of so-called regredience and Winnicott's account of "imaginative elaboration", and how he applied that in his therapeutic consultations. In his introduction to *Therapeutic Consultations in Child Psychiatry* (1971) he describes the Squiggle game, a game with no rules and regulations, as simply a way of getting in contact with a child where "there is a need in the child which will show in the course of time in the setting which I can provide". He observes how often a child will come to the consultation having had a dream the night before in which he, Winnicott, figured. He plays with the possibility that for the child he is *a subjective object*, created but already there to be found, conjured up to reach that "something", alluding to the infant's original "creation" of the mother through illusion. If this opportunity can be used because the child meets in the analyst an alive available object, then deep work can be done, resulting in "the loosening of the knot and forward movement in the developmental process" (p. 5); the patient gradually surprises himself by the production of ideas and feelings that have not been previously integrated into the total personality. The basis of the process is playing and draws upon the analyst having free enough access to his or her own imagination, rooted in the psyche/soma, but integrated with, not dominated by mind: intellectual thought.

Winnicott is using here a different metaphor, a textile or yarn, which is knotted; not a rent or hole in the fabric; variations on the same theme ... and if we look closely at his work then we can see he is in the same territory.

The case of Bob

I will summarise this case which was first published in the *International Journal of Psychoanalysis* as part of the festschrift for Heinz Hartmann (Winnicott, 1965).

Six-year-old Bob was brought by his parents because of his so-called "primary defect", a learning disability including retardation of speech, thus a problem with his mind perhaps rooted in the coexistent problem with his psyche, each, as we will see, connected to the failure in environmental provision in his early life. Winnicott didn't know Bob's history before the therapeutic consultation but was told it following, and I will do the same. I am going to show the squiggle slides and some of DWW's comments about them.

The child could not be seen for analysis but the consultation enabled what DWW described as "this complex organization round a traumatic event [to] become transformed into material that can be forgotten because it has been remembered".

(Drawings at the end of this chapter)

It takes a little while for Bob to get the sense of the game but from the start (drawing 1) DWW doubts the diagnosis of primary defect. Bob adds eyes to DWW's squiggle at drawing 6 and calls it "Humpty Dumpty" (who had a great fall and couldn't be put back together again). He repeatedly and increasingly adds eyes, several times blackened. Other images include in drawing 9 the maze, accompanied by rapid panicky speech; a jet plane that might go upside down; and a big mountain down which he might slip because it's all ice. His "awful dream" emerges after drawing 23 about a witch who makes him disappear (smudged-in eyes), vanish, and the chaos in drawing 24 is accompanied by "his dramatising horror and his penis got excited and he screwed himself up because of anxiety". At drawing 25 he draws himself in bed having a nightmare and then tells DWW of falling downstairs but Daddy was there and took him to Mummy.

A sense of crescendo is conveyed and DWW says: "I now had the clearest possible evidence of Bob's wish to tell me about a lapse in environmental provision which had been otherwise good in a general way. I therefore started to talk and I drew."

He drew a full picture (drawing 26) of the mother holding the baby in her arms whom he then scribbles out. Bob at that point took the paper and smudged in the woman's eyes at the same time saying, "She goes to sleep." DWW drew the baby on the floor "wondering how Bob would deal with the archaic anxiety associated with falling forever". Bob then said, "No, the witch came when the mother shut her eyes. I just screamed. I saw the witch; Mummy saw the witch; I shouted, "My Mummy will get you." Mummy saw the witch, Daddy was downstairs and he took his penknife and stuck it into the witch's tummy so it got killed for ever."

In this variation in the setting, the image, replete with affective quality is both the conduit through which experience is represented, and constitutes the analytic encounter. DWW describes the Squiggle game as containing "an impulsive moment ... mad unless done by a sane person which is why some children find them frightening .... Their form and content can be incontinent and thus naughty for some children." He adds that the *integration* that is in each squiggle comes from *his* contribution and when the resultant squiggle is "satisfactory" it is like a "found object, for instance a stone or a piece of wood that a sculptor may find and set up as a kind of expression". The integration is his soma-psyche-mind at work creating and finding the stone or piece of wood that gives form, representation, to the child's experience conveyed through the affective, imagistic encounter. In her very interesting article, "Squiggle Evidence" in *Donald Winnicott Today* (2013) Lisa Farley describes his interest in the provision of experience where "someone who could witness and acknowledge 'instinctual urges including aggressive ones' as grounds for symbolisation, imagination and creativity" (p. 426 referring to DWW's "Children in the War" broadcast, 1940).

The images are co-created and DWW is free to fashion a meaningful narrative of Bob's internal predicament now presented in their joint productions. The analyst's contribution is from "his own ingenuity"; and his internal freedom "has a great importance for the success". DWW introduces the game to the child as one which he likes, thus inviting the child to share something enjoyable from him, an expression of his libidinal investment in the process. I am reminded of the earlier quotation from Andre Green.

Through the narrative created in this encounter Bob's early trauma emerged. We learn it began soon after birth with his hospitalisation for two weeks at fourteen days old for pyloric stenosis, thus a radical early separation from his mother, and reinforced by her emotional absence into postnatal depression when he was fourteen months old after his baby brother was born. The primary manifestation of that depression was her falling asleep on the sofa: the black closed eyes; a depression that became chronic. It is that disappearance, or her decathexis, that is now re-presented or represented for the first time, in the drawings with the inserted black eyes. The indications of unintegrated, early trauma of separation are in the image of the jet plane in which he might go upside-down. The theme of falling recurs many times, alluding to profound anxieties of the most fundamental kind: falling forever, annihilation. "The content of No. 21 made me prepared for a new version of environmental failure producing threat of primitive anxiety of the type of falling, depersonalization, confusion, disorientation, etc." Bob was described as "obviously tied to his mother", perhaps unable to leave her as he had been psychically left, or in Green's terms had taken up residence at the tomb of the dead mother. However, all this had been overlain with something else, referred to in a comment of the generally good environmental provision, though with gaps. The range of his interests (space, God, life and death) eventually led to some questioning of whether Bob was really "simple". We are also told that his IQ on the Stanford-Binet assessment placed him within the normal range, although slightly low. He couldn't use his mind because of the rent or gap in his psyche, and this is where Winnicott met him.

Closing remarks

So let us see where we have got to. I have focused on one aspect of so-called regression as it is being conceived in contemporary psychanalysis: the Botellas' translation to "regredience" of topographical regression, which is intended to get away from any pathological associations to the concept. Following Rycroft, and using DWW's model of the soma/psyche/mind, I see the analyst's integration of this triad as the source of her imaginative elaboration of her experience of her patient, not necessarily a regressive process. In situations of early relational trauma this capacity is needed to give representational form, or as the Botellas refer to it, figurability, where hitherto there has been none. Work with children demonstrates it particularly clearly because of the method: the use of drawings, stories, toys, sensory elements of play. But it is probably always a central feature of what the analyst draws upon in order to give form to the unconscious. In certain circumstances as I hope I have shown, it is not the repressed which now re-emerges, but for the first time unintegrated experiences are given form, representation and thus are available for the ordinary exigencies of psychic and mental life.

104 DONALD W. WINNICOTT AND THE HISTORY OF THE PRESENT

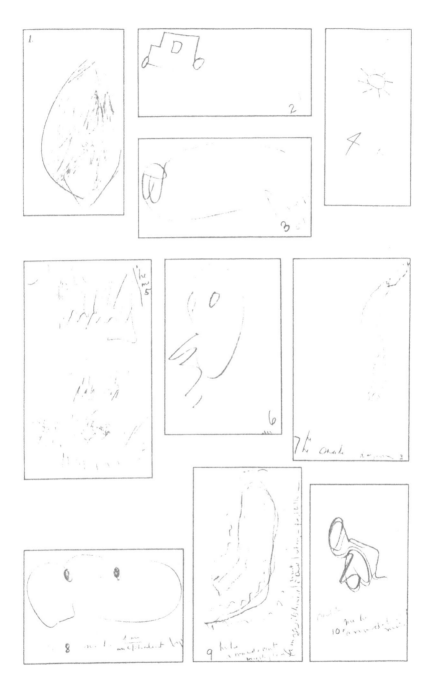

IMAGES AND WORDS 105

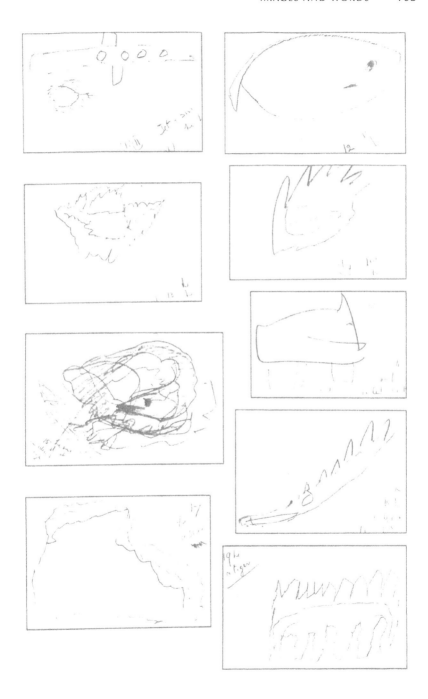

| Omitted. Bob's writing of his name (one consonant reversed) and the figure 6 (he could not spell 'six'), his age. 20 |  |  |

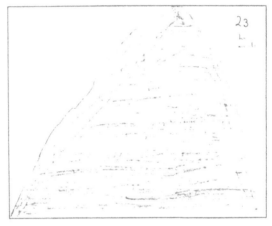

IMAGES AND WORDS 107

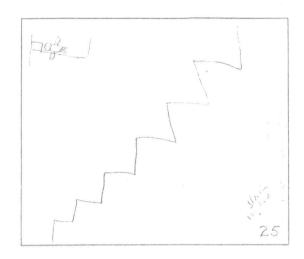

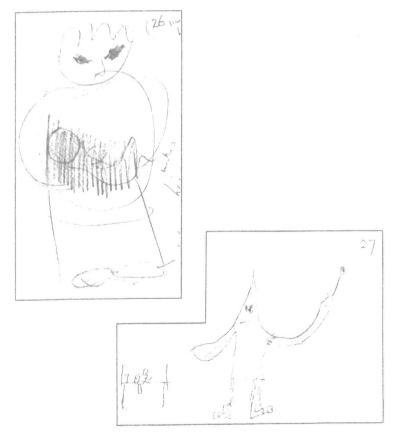

Notes

1. With thanks to Coretta Samms.
2. With thanks to Flavia Ansaldo.

References

Alvarez, A. (1992). *Live Company: Psychoanalytic Psychotherapy with Autistic, Borderline Deprived and Abused Children*. London: Routledge.
Alvarez, A. (2012). *The Thinking Heart*. Hove, UK: Routledge.
Balint, M. (1968). *The Basic Fault*. London: Tavistock.
Botella, C., & Botella, S. (2005). *The Work of Psychic Figurability: on Mental States without Representation*. London: New Library of Psychoanalysis and Routledge.
Botella, C., & Botella, S. (2013). Psychic figurability and unrepresented states. In: H. Levine, G. Reid, & D. Scarfone (Eds.), *Unrepresented States and the Construction of Meaning*. London: Karnac.
Farley, L. (2013). Squiggle evidence: the child, the canvas, and the "negative labour" of writing history. In: J. Abram (Ed.), *Donald Winnicott Today* (Chapter 18, pp. 418–452). London: New Library of Psychoanalysis and Routledge.
Ferenczi, S. (1931). Child analysis in the analysis of adults. *International Journal of Psychoanalysis, 12*: 468–482.
Freud, S. (1900a). *The Interpretation of Dreams*. S. E., 5: 509–610. London: Hogarth.
Green, A. (1980). The dead mother. In: *On Private Madness* (pp. 142–173). London: Hogarth and the Institute of Psychoanalysis, 1986.
Lanyado, M. (2004). *The Presence of the Therapist: Treating Childhood Trauma*. Hove, UK: Brunner Routledge.
Rycroft, C. (1981). *The Innocence of Dreams*. Oxford: Oxford University Press.
Winnicott, D. W. (1949). Mind and its relation to psyche-soma. In: *Collected Papers: Through Paediatrics to Psycho-Analysis, Second edition* (pp. 243–254). London: Hogarth and the Institute of Psychoanalysis, 1958.
Winnicott, D. W. (1954a). Metapsychological and clinical aspects of regression within the psycho-analytical set-up. In: *Collected Papers: Through Paediatrics to Psycho-Analysis, Second edition*. London: Hogarth and the Institute of Psychoanalysis, 1958.
Winnicott, D. W. (1954b). Withdrawal and regression. In: *Collected Papers: Through Paediatrics to Psycho-Analysis, Second edition* (pp. 255–261). London: Hogarth and the Institute of Psychoanalysis, 1958.

Winnicott, D. W. (1965). A clinical study of the effects of a failure of the average expectable environment on a child's mental functioning. *International Journal of Psychoanalysis, 46*: 41–87.

Winnicott, D. W. (1970). Residential care as therapy. In: C. Winnicott, R. Shepherd, & M. Davis (Eds.), *Deprivation and Delinquency* (pp. 220–228). London: Tavistock, 1984.

Winnicott, D. W. (1971). *Therapeutic Consultations in Child Psychiatry*. London: Hogarth and the Institute of Psychoanalysis.

CHAPTER NINE

The public psychoanalyst: Donald Winnicott as broadcaster

Brett Kahr

> "I am not afraid to speak in public"—
> Winston Churchill, 1891, at Harrow School,
> quoted by fellow Harrovian, Sir Murland Evans, 2nd Baronet Evans of Tubbendeny
>
> (quoted in Gilbert, 1994, p. 215)

Psychoanalysis has never enjoyed a particularly comfortable relationship with the general public.

In view of the fact that psychoanalytical clinicians practise the most private of professions, it should not be at all surprising that members of the Freudian community invariably struggle over such basic issues as whether we can publish our case material; whether we can speak about our work in any detail beyond the confines of training institutions; and whether we can appear on radio or television. Mental health professionals often debate if "outreach" to the general public constitutes a worthy contribution to the dissemination of psychological knowledge or if it represents, by contrast, an ethical breach.

Sigmund Freud certainly regarded journalists and filmmakers with considerable suspicion. Famously, the father of psychoanalysis refused to meet with the Hollywood mogul Samuel Goldwyn, who had invited

Freud to participate in the planning of a film about the great lovers in history (Jones, 1957). Similarly, Freud declined a lucrative invitation to serve as an expert witness in the famous American murder trial of the young assassins Nathan Leopold, Jr. and Richard Loeb (Baatz, 2008; Kahr, 2005, 2007; Seldes, 1953). Furthermore, Freud expressed strong reservations about Georg Wilhelm Pabst's pioneering film about psychoanalysis, *Geheimnisse einer Seele* (Secrets of a Soul), and he became most displeased when he discovered that several of his disciples had become consultants to this cinematic project (e.g., Freud, 1925; cp. Chodorkoff & Baxter, 1974; Ries, 1995).

In Great Britain, psychoanalysts did not engage with the media particularly well during the first half of the twentieth century (e.g., Rapp, 1988, 1990). Indeed, the British Broadcasting Corporation banned Dr Ernest Jones from appearing on air due to the controversial reputation of Freudianism; indeed, as Jones (1932, p. 694) explained, the BBC had placed his name "on a black list as a morally dangerous person" (cf. Jones, 1957; Maddox, 2006). And when Dr John Rickman (1935), another pioneering British psychoanalyst, offered to speak on the radio, the BBC rejected his services, as the broadcasting staff found the sound of his speaking voice to be quite "unsuitable" (cp. Kahr, 2013).

Thus, when Dr Donald Winnicott embarked upon his pioneering radio talks for the BBC during the late 1930s and early 1940s, he broke new ground by transmitting psychologically orientated ideas to literally millions of Britons. In this respect, he succeeded in promulgating the ethos of Freudianism with greater success than virtually any other mental health professional had ever done previously.

Winnicott's path-breaking broadcasts on radio, as well as his written contributions for magazines, not to mention his many lectures to members of the general public, required great courage and skill. Not only did Winnicott possess a remarkable speaking voice—perfect for the airwaves—but, also, he withstood the disapprobation of his psychoanalytical colleagues for speaking outside the Freudian milieu (Kahr, 2002; MacCarthy, 2002, 2005). Furthermore, he endured the barbs of psychiatric colleagues who objected to his public espousal of psychoanalytical ideas (e.g., Millar, 1947; Young, 1947).

But in spite of raised eyebrows, if not outright resistance, Donald Winnicott proved deeply effective as a psychological broadcaster, and he persevered with this work for the rest of his career, appearing frequently on radio throughout the 1940s, 1950s, and 1960s; and latterly, he became one of the first psychoanalysts ever to participate in a television broadcast! Indeed, Winnicott's remarks about mothers and babies proved quite deeply therapeutic to his listeners. For instance, during the bombings of the Second World War, a certain Mrs Helen Trevelyan (1944) wrote to Winnicott that, "At a very bleak moment I turned on the wireless + heard your voice—you can imagine how it sustained me!"

Fortunately, not all of the members of the psychoanalytical community expressed disapproval at Winnicott's efforts to publicise psychological ideas. Dr. Ernest Jones (1944), then retired and very much a beneficent grandee, could enjoy the fact that Winnicott, a long-term protégé, had undertaken such important work. With generosity, Jones (1944) wrote to Winnicott: "I have been reading with great pleasure the broadcast you kindly sent me, which at the time I unfortunately missed. It is really charming and brings out to the full your wonderful gift of empathy. I am sure it must have benefitted many people."

Similarly, the members of his family of origin, namely, his widowed father Sir Frederick Winnicott, and his sisters Violet and Kathleen, supported Donald Winnicott with unrestricted affection. During the 1940s, Violet Winnicott (n.d.), his elder sister, wrote, "We 'listened in' at 10.45 with rapt attention. Father + Kathleen recognised your voice. I didn't think it *was* you. It sounded like *your* words read by someone else. It came through perfectly +, as K said "It was a little jewel of a broadcast." Perfect in every way. Father's wireless has gone wrong, so we had to fix up our old set, which probably made your voice sound different."

After completing a raft of wartime broadcasts, Winnicott's yen for working in the media and in public education persisted, and on January 24, 1949, having listened to a BBC radio programme on the role of leucotomy (lobotomy) in the treatment of mental illness, he sent an unsolicited letter to Miss Isa Benzie, a pioneering female radio producer. He wrote:

> Dear Miss Benzie,
>
> I wonder if you remember me? You were very kind to me when I was giving the talks about Parents and Children, and you came to the British Psychological Society Medical Section when I read a paper there in which I expressed criticism of electric shock therapy and leucotomy. Do you remember that at the time you asked me whether I would

be willing to talk on the wireless on this subject? At the time I refused because I felt that it would be better to work in psychiatric circles and not to introduce the subject to the wider public for fear of rousing emotion and making the scientific discussion more difficult. (1949b)

Explaining that he had spent more time of late thinking about potential broadcasting projects, he wondered whether "… there is now a place wide open for a talk by someone who feels that the tendency represented by leucotomy is a bad one, and one which the public should interest themselves in and have an opinion on. I should be most grateful if you would put me in touch with the right department, or actually put in a word for me to find out whether I could be asked to state my personal view" (1949b).

Miss Benzie replied to Dr Winnicott's letter the very next day, expressing a wish to discuss Winnicott's broadcasting ideas more fully. On January 26, 1949, Winnicott (1949c) responded that, "Broadcasts about children really interest me four thousand times more than broadcasts about the frontal lobes." Soon thereafter, Winnicott and Benzie met in person, and she became instantly captivated by his notion of the ordinary devoted mother, and swiftly commissioned him to undertake a further set of talks (Winnicott, 1949a).

Nearly two decades later, Winnicott (1966, pp. 3–4) reminisced about this pivotal meeting with Isa Benzie:

> She was, of course, on the lookout for a catchphrase, but I did not know this. I told her that I had no interest whatever in trying to tell people what to do. To start with, I didn't know. But I would like to talk to mothers about the thing that they do well, and that they do well simply because each mother is devoted to the task in hand, namely the care of one infant, or perhaps twins. I said that ordinarily this just happens, and it is the exception when a baby has to do without being cared for at the start by a specialist. Isa Benzie picked up the clue in a matter of twenty yards, and she said: "Splendid! The Ordinary Devoted Mother." So that was that.

Winnicott's radio broadcasts and his writings for such popular publications as *The New Era in Home and School*, *The Times*, *The Spectator*, and *New Society* consolidated his reputation as a public spokesperson for psychological ideas, and helped to demystify the monastic retreat cultivated by many psychoanalysts at that time (e.g., 1941, 1945a, 1945d, 1945e, 1945f, 1950, 1954, 1963, 1965, 1967a, 1967b). And of course, Winnicott's work in the field now known as "media psychology" reached its apotheosis with the appearance of his landmark book *The Child, the Family, and the Outside World* (1964), an amalgamation of his two earlier books *The Child and the Family: First Relationships* (1957a) and *The Child and the Outside World: Studies in Developing Relationships* (1957b). Published by Penguin Books, Winnicott's 1964 omnibus edition became an undisputed best-seller, perhaps the first British psychoanalytical book to achieve such a status; and it has, of course, remained in print ever since.

While other psychoanalysts of the immediate pre-war and post-war period wrote copiously about valuable specialist, technical clinical topics, Winnicott (who also penned articles about such professional matters) succeeded in broadcasting and publishing on such simple, direct, and valuable notions as "Why Children Play" (1942), "Getting to Know Your Baby" (1945b), "Why Do Babies Cry?" (1945c), "Neglected Children" (1950), and so many more. In this respect, he created a new audience, something that the towering figures of Anna Freud, Melanie Klein, and others never did, in spite of their venerable achievements within the psychoanalytical community.

Sadly, apart from the occasional pat on the back from Ernest Jones, Winnicott received little encouragement of his media work from his fellow psychoanalysts. Fortunately, the roots of Donald Winnicott's capacities as the first truly public psychoanalyst did not stem from or, indeed, depend upon collegial support but derived unsurprisingly from his early childhood experiences.

Long before Winnicott underwent any emboldening personal psychoanalyses with James Strachey and, years later, with Joan Riviere, he had the benefit of growing up in a family whose members led very confident public lives. Both his father, Frederick Winnicott, and his uncle, Richard Winnicott, served as mayor of the town of Plymouth (Kahr, 1996); and in this capacity, they chaired large meetings, opened buildings, made speeches, walked in ceremonial parades wearing their chain of office, and much more besides (Kahr, 2015). Winnicott's mother, Elizabeth Martha Woods Winnicott, likewise, played an important role in civic life, and helped to establish a support group for young mothers (Kahr, 2017). Thus, Winnicott spent his formative years surrounded by close family members who had no restrictions or inhibitions about sharing their capacities and knowledge with the members of their large, local community.

But Donald Winnicott's facility as a broadcaster emerged not only from identification with family members but, also, from other more ancient roots. When the magazine editor Peggy Volkov (1944) wrote to Winnicott, expostulating that, "Your BBC stuff is as simple as the gospel stories," she may not have fully appreciated Winnicott's deep immersion in religion.

The Winnicotts of Plymouth, a family of devout and liberal Christians, practised in the tradition of Wesleyan Methodism. Indeed, John Wesley, the founder of English Methodism, maintained a strong belief in communicating Christian precepts of love and charity to the widest possible audience; and during his lifetime as a preacher he delivered many open-air sermons to extremely large numbers of people, often 40,000 or 50,000 at a time (Pudney, 1978; cp. Ayling, 1979; Baker, 1970; Brailsford, 1954; Simon, 1925). In retrospect, one might regard the eighteenth-century Wesley as a pioneer "broadcaster" of his era. As a boy, Donald Winnicott attended Wesleyan Methodist church services on a frequent basis (Kahr, 1996; Neve, 1983; C. Winnicott, 1978); and consequently, he absorbed much of its outward focus.

But Winnicott also derived much "broadcasting" inspiration from the Lollards, a sect of medieval English Nonconformists who flourished in the fourteenth and fifteenth centuries and who protested against the strictures of Catholicism, long before Henry VIII's revolt in the sixteenth century which resulted in the dissolution of the monasteries. The Lollards objected to many features of ritualised English Catholicism, not least the reliance upon preaching in Latin as opposed to the vernacular. Their spiritual leader, the theologian John Wycliffe, argued that the Bible should be rendered in ordinary English so that it could be read not only by clergymen but, also, by uneducated English men and women. The Lollards evoked the wrath of many Catholic clergymen, not least Archbishop Thomas Arundel, who condemned the English-language tracts of the Lollards as dangerous "libros suspectos in lingua vulgari Anglicana" (quoted in Hudson, 1972, p. 156).

Winnicott maintained a long-standing identification with these Lollard heretics who risked their lives to transmit theology to the masses. Indeed, as he wrote in later years to the dramatist Ian Rodger, "My feeling is that I am a natural Lollard and would have had a bad time in the 14th and 15th centuries" (1969). He underscored that "[T]he Lollards laid the basis for liberal thinking in England and Europe" (1969). In many respects, one might come to regard Donald Winnicott as a cross between a Wesleyan open-air preacher and a medieval Lollard heretic who spoke in plain language. Indeed, while many psychoanalytical colleagues relished a Greco-Latin vocabulary of complex terms ranging from "cathexis" and "superego" to "libido" and "parapraxis", Winnicott created a body of jargon-free radio broadcasts and magazine articles which could be read and enjoyed by the populace at large.

Throughout a long and distinguished clinical career, Donald Winnicott made a wealth of contributions as a theoretician, a technician, a teacher, a supervisor, an administrator, an author, and so much more. Indeed, in view of the fact that he bequeathed so many rich jewels to our profession, one would be hard pressed to identify his *most* important accomplishment. But amid the many achievements of Donald Winnicott, we do him a great disservice if we marginalise, or indeed obliterate, his profound work as a pioneer of mental health broadcasting in Great Britain and beyond. In an era dominated by biological psychiatry and short-term cognitive-behavioural therapies, the dynamic therapies need bold, clear, brave spokesmen and spokeswomen who have the temerity to follow in Winnicott's footsteps, and who can, with modesty and, also, with confidence, transmit the best of the culture of the dynamic talking cure to the world beyond the consulting room.

References

Ayling, S. (1979). *John Wesley*. London: William Collins.
Baatz, S. (2008). *For the Thrill of It: Leopold, Loeb, and the Murder that Shocked Chicago*. New York: Harper/HarperCollins.
Baker, F. (1970). *John Wesley and the Church of England*. London: Epworth.
Benzie, I. D. (1949). Letter to Donald W. Winnicott. January 25. PP/DWW/B/B/5/1. Donald Woods Winnicott Collection. Archives and Manuscripts, Rare Materials Room, Wellcome Library, Wellcome Collection, The Wellcome Building, London.
Brailsford, M. R. (1954). *A Tale of Two Brothers: John and Charles Wesley*. London: Rupert Hart-Davis.
Chodorkoff, B., & Baxter, S. (1974). "Secrets of a Soul": An early psychoanalytic film venture. *American Imago, 31*: 319–334.
Freud, S. (1925). Letter to Karl Abraham. June 9. In: E. Falzeder & L. M. Hermanns (Eds.), *Sigmund Freud und Karl Abraham* (2009). *Briefwechsel*

1907–1925: Vollständige Ausgabe. Band 2: 1915–1925 (pp. 823–824). Vienna: Turia und Kant.

Gilbert, M. (1994). *In Search of Churchill: A Historian's Journey*. London: HarperCollins.

Hudson, A. (1972). Some aspects of Lollard book production. In: D. Baker (Ed.), *Schism, Heresy and Religious Protest: Papers Read at the Tenth Summer Meeting and the Eleventh Winter Meeting of the Ecclesiastical History Society* (pp. 147–157). Cambridge: Cambridge University Press.

Jones, E. (1932). Letter to Sigmund Freud. May 5. In: R. A. Paskauskas (Ed.), Sigmund Freud and Ernest Jones (1993). *The Complete Correspondence of Sigmund Freud and Ernest Jones: 1908–1939* (pp. 694–695). Cambridge, MA: Belknap Press of Harvard University Press.

Jones, E. (1944). Letter to Donald W. Winnicott. January 26. PP/DWW/B/A/16. Donald Woods Winnicott Collection. Archives and Manuscripts, Rare Materials Room, Wellcome Library, Wellcome Collection, The Wellcome Building, London.

Jones, E. (1957). *The Life and Work of Sigmund Freud: Volume 3. The Last Phase. 1919–1939*. New York: Basic Books.

Kahr, B. (1996). *D. W. Winnicott: A Biographical Portrait*. London: Karnac.

Kahr, B. (2002). Interview with Brendan MacCarthy. July 24.

Kahr, B. (2005). Why Freud turned down $25,000: Mental health professionals in the witness box. *American Imago, 62*: 365–371.

Kahr, B. (2007). Why Freud turned down $25,000. In: J. Ryan (Ed.), *Tales of Psychotherapy* (pp. 5–9). London: Karnac.

Kahr, B. (2013). Media monasticism and media whoredom: the uncomfortable marriage between psychoanalysis and public exposure. Unpublished typescript.

Kahr, B. (2015). The Roots of Mental Health Broadcasting. Afternoon Workshop on "Donald Winnicott, the Public Psychoanalyst: Broadcasting Beyond the Consulting Room". International Conference on "Donald Winnicott and the History of the Present: A Celebration of the Collected Works of D. W. Winnicott". The Winnicott Trust, London, in association with the British Psychoanalytical Society, London, and the British Psychoanalytic Association, British Psychotherapy Foundation, London, and the Association of Independent Psychoanalysts, London, at the Board Room, Mary Ward House Conference and Exhibition Centre, Holborn, London. November 21.

Kahr, B. (2017). *Untitled Biography of Donald Woods Winnicott*. (In preparation.)

MacCarthy, B. (2002). Personal communication to the author. July 17.

MacCarthy, B. (2005). Personal communication to the author. March 16.

Maddox, B. (2006). *Freud's Wizard: The Enigma of Ernest Jones*. London: John Murray/Hodder Headline.

Millar, W. M. (1947). Physical therapy of mental disorder. *British Medical Journal*, June 14: 861.

Neve, M. (1983). Interview with Clare Winnicott, June. In: P. L. Rudnytsky, *The Psychoanalytic Vocation: Rank, Winnicott, and the Legacy of Freud* (pp. 180–193). New Haven, CT: Yale University Press, 1991.

Pudney, J. (1978). *John Wesley and His World*. London: Thames & Hudson.

Rapp, D. (1988). The reception of Freud by the British press: general interest and literary magazines, 1920–1925. *Journal of the History of the Behavioral Sciences*, 24: 191–201.

Rapp, D. (1990). The early discovery of Freud by the British general educated public, 1912–1919. *Social History of Medicine*, 3: 217–243.

Rickman, J. (1935). Letter to Roger Money-Kyrle. June 26. PP/RMK/C.1. Roger Ernle Money-Kyrle (1898–1980), psychoanalyst Collection. Archives and Manuscripts, Rare Materials Room, Wellcome Library, Wellcome Collection, The Wellcome Building, London.

Ries, P. (1995). Popularise and/or be damned: Psychoanalysis and film at the crossroads in 1925. *International Journal of Psychoanalysis*, 76: 759–791.

Seldes, G. (1953). *Tell the Truth and Run*. New York: Greenberg: Publisher.

Simon, J. S. (1925). *John Wesley and the Advance of Methodism*. London: Epworth Press/J. Alfred Sharp.

Trevelyan, H. (1944). Letter to Donald W. Winnicott. December 16. PP/DWW/B/A/29. Donald Woods Winnicott Collection. Archives and Manuscripts, Rare Materials Room, Wellcome Library, Wellcome Collection, The Wellcome Building, London.

Volkov, P. (1944). Letter to Donald W. Winnicott. May 25. PP/DWW/B/B/5/4. Donald Woods Winnicott Collection. Archives and Manuscripts, Rare Materials Room, Wellcome Library, Wellcome Collection, The Wellcome Building, London.

Winnicott, C. (1978). D. W. W.: A reflection. In: S. A. Grolnick, L. Barkin, & W. Muensterberger (Eds.), *Between Reality and Fantasy: Transitional Objects and Phenomena* (pp. 17–33). New York: Jason Aronson.

Winnicott, D. W. (1941). On influencing and being influenced. *New Era in Home and School*, 22: 118–120.

Winnicott, D. W. (1942). Why children play. *New Era in Home and School*, 23: 12–14.

Winnicott, D. W. (1945a). *Getting to Know Your Baby*. London: William Heinemann (Medical Books).

Winnicott, D. W. (1945b). Getting to know your baby. *New Era in Home and School*, 26: 1–3.

Winnicott, D. W. (1945c). Why do babies cry? *New Era in Home and School*, 26: 3, 5–7.
Winnicott, D. W. (1945d). Infant feeding. *New Era in Home and School*, 26: 9–10.
Winnicott, D. W. (1945e). What about father? *New Era in Home and School*, 26: 11–13.
Winnicott, D. W. (1945f). Their standards and yours. *New Era in Home and School*, 26: 13–15.
Winnicott, D. W. (1949a). *The Ordinary Devoted Mother and Her Baby: Nine Broadcast Talks (Autumn 1949)*. London: C. A. Brock.
Winnicott, D. W. (1949b). Letter to Isa D. Benzie. January 24. PP/DWW/B/B/5/1. Donald Woods Winnicott Collection. Archives and Manuscripts, Rare Materials Room, Wellcome Library, Wellcome Collection, The Wellcome Building, London.
Winnicott, D. W. (1949c). Letter to Isa D. Benzie. January 26. PP/DWW/B/B/5/1. Donald Woods Winnicott Collection. Archives and Manuscripts, Rare Materials Room, Wellcome Library, Wellcome Collection, The Wellcome Building, London.
Winnicott, D. W. (1950). Neglected children. *The Times*. January 31, p. 5.
Winnicott, D. W. (1954). A psychiatrist's choice. *The Spectator*. February 12: 175.
Winnicott, D. W. (1957a). *The Child and the Family: First Relationships*. J. Hardenberg (Ed.). London: Tavistock.
Winnicott, D. W. (1957b). *The Child and the Outside World: Studies in Developing Relationships*. J. Hardenberg (Ed.). London: Tavistock.
Winnicott, D. W. (1963). Struggling through the doldrums. *New Society*. April 25: 8–11.
Winnicott, D. W. (1964). *The Child, the Family, and the Outside World*. London: Penguin.
Winnicott, D. W. (1965). Acknowledge the difference. *New Society*. September 9: 29.
Winnicott, D. W. (1966). The ordinary devoted mother. In: C. Winnicott, R. Shepherd, & M. Davis (Eds.), *Babies and Their Mothers* (pp. 3–14). Reading, MA: Addison-Wesley.
Winnicott, D. W. (1967a). Steps to good parenthood. *New Society*. April 13: 545–546.
Winnicott, D. W. (1967b). The persecution that wasn't. *New Society*. May 25: 772–773.
Winnicott, D. W. (1969). Letter to Ian Rodger. May 28. Box 7. File 16. Donald W. Winnicott Papers. Archives of Psychiatry, The Oskar Diethelm Library, The DeWitt Wallace Institute for the History of Psychiatry,

Department of Psychiatry, Joan and Sanford I. Weill Medical College, Cornell University, The New York Presbyterian Hospital, New York.

Winnicott, V. (n.d.). Letter to Donald W. Winnicott. n.d. PP/DWW/B/D/3. Donald Woods Winnicott Collection. Archives and Manuscripts, Rare Materials Room, Wellcome Library, Wellcome Collection, The Wellcome Building, London.

Young, M. L. (1947). Physical therapy of mental disorder. *British Medical Journal*, July 5: 32–33.

CHAPTER TEN

Beyond the consulting room: Winnicott the broadcaster*

Anne Karpf

Between 1943 and 1962, the psychoanalyst Donald Winnicott gave more than fifty broadcasts on BBC Radio. Mostly taking the form of scripted talks, they covered a wide range of subjects—from guilt and jealousy to evacuation and step-parents—and later formed the basis of a bestselling book—*The Child, the Family and the Outside World*, first published in 1964, and two other volumes, *Talking to Parents* (1993) and *Winnicott on the Child* (2002). They began life as radio broadcasts, however—most famously the series "The Ordinary Devoted Mother and Her Baby" (1949–52).

In these talks Winnicott laid out the fundamentals of his theory: that the baby is a person from the start, that it is through the intimate relationship with an attentive, "devoted", "good enough" mother—a mother who can be loved, hated, and depended upon—that the baby develops into a healthy, independent, adult individual. And that when mothers try to do things by the book—or by the wireless—"[T]hey lose

---

*This paper is based on a longer article, "Constructing and Addressing the 'Ordinary Devoted Mother': Donald Winnicott's BBC broadcasts, 1943–62", published in *History Workshop Journal*, vol. 78, Autumn 2014, with thanks for permission to reproduce parts of it here.

touch with their own ability to act without knowing exactly what is right and what is wrong" (Winnicott, 1993, p. 5). On the other hand, "When things go wrong, as they must do from time to time, you are at a disadvantage if you are working blind. If you know what's going on you become less sensitive to criticism and to chance remarks from passers-by" (Winnicott, 2002, p. 131)—the raison d'etre of his talks.

Adam Phillips (1988) has argued that for Winnicott, the non-prescriptive mother in her relationship to the baby formed a model for the non-impinging psychoanalyst—both of them creating a setting of trust in which development could take place at its own pace. In some sense Winnicott extended this same practice to the broadcast, hoping to engender in the listener not compliance but a space in which to think about her baby and his needs. Winnicott provided a "holding environment" for listeners, and his producers provided a holding environment for him.

Winnicott's broadcasting career was shaped by two pioneering female producers in the BBC's Talks Department, Janet Quigley and Isa Benzie, from whom he was eager to learn and remarkably open to criticism. Winnicott's talks are often described as though they were somehow pre-existing and simply needed to be "decanted" onto the wireless. Nothing could be further from the truth. Janet Quigley and later Isa Benzie were formative in guiding both the choice of subject matter and approach, and in ensuring that he didn't make listeners feel guilty.

What is remarkable is how quickly he established himself. He started broadcasting only in 1943 and yet by 1946 Isa Benzie, discussing a project, declared: "We think the programme is likely to stand or fall by your participation."[1] By 1949 he had carte blanche in his choice of subject matter. He was also learning to think like a broadcaster—which ideas would work on air, how many talks they would need, and even how topical they were. Yet Winnicott never stopped being self-critical and tried, to the last, to develop his skills as a broadcaster. In 1945 he wrote to Quigley: "Use the blue pencil or any other colour. Or say if it's no good."[2]

The new cultural form of the radio talk suited him beautifully. In 1933 Hilda Matheson, director of Talks at the BBC, had urged broadcasters not "to address the microphone as if it were a public meeting … The person sitting at the other end expected the speaker to address him [sic] personally, simply, almost familiarly, as man to man" (Matheson, 1933, pp. 75–76). Winnicott managed to sound simultaneously authoritative and (relatively) conversational. Unlike many of his colleagues, who regarded broadcasting as an exercise in narcissism or exhibitionism, or feared (as Anna Freud did) that appearing on the radio would seem like advertising their services, he did not believe that popularising diminished the seriousness of his work.

One factor contributing to his success as a broadcaster was the clear conception he had of his listeners. Winnicott believed it was to mothers that he "deeply needed to speak" (Winnicott,1986, p.123), and one of his most powerful stylistic devices was to address them in the second person, as "you". "You will be relieved", he reassured them, "that I am not going to tell you what to do … I cannot tell you exactly what to do but I can talk about what it all means" (1964, pp. 15–16).

Winnicott had an acute understanding of different audiences, and the different registers they called for. He had no hesitation in writing outspoken and provocative letters to the *British Medical Journal* on controversial subjects like ECT, leucotomy, and evacuation, but on radio his tone was always non-judgemental. He intuitively understood the dangers of focusing, to an undifferentiated radio audience, on the pathological rather than the ordinary, especially because it brought the risk that listeners would feel bad but would have no access to therapy. And from his earliest broadcasts onwards, they wrote to him in great numbers, occasionally "fiercely critical"[3] but more often highly appreciative, praising the fact that, as one listener put it, "He holds no one guilty."[4]

He was helped by his strong sense of when to use psychoanalytic terms and when to translate them into a demotic language accessible to lay listeners. So, for example, in his 1960 broadcast "What Irks", he was able to allude to the argument he made in his paper "Hate in the Countertransference" without ever using the clinical term (Winnicott, 1993, p. 75) and in the 1962 talk "Now We Are Five", he describes the transitional object as a "special object" (Winnicott, 1993, p. 118).

Winnicott could describe phenomena that were "outside the realm of the written or spoken word until he came to grips with them" (Rodman, 2003, p. 44). He came up with arresting phrases—such as "good enough mother"—which then became part of both specialist and popular discourse (Schwartz, 1999). He was also a famously playful communicator. Benjamin Spock praised "… the surprising contrasts in his language. It is predominantly grave, deeply thoughtful and analytical. Then suddenly he gives way to earthy folk talk" (2002, p. 7). He had an instinctive feel for what has been described as "the curious fusion of these two technologies of dislocated identity ... ether and unconscious" (Sconce, 2009, p. 33).

Through his broadcasting experience, Winnicott developed the skill of writing to speak. The published versions of his scripts hardly needed editing (C. Winnicott, Bollas, Davis, & Shepherd, 1993, p. xvi). Paragraphs added by hand in the studio to his scripts are as fluent as any of his other writing. Winnicott wrote words that he could speak easily on air, and his scripts were then published—the cycle from written to oral back to written forms reflected the fact that he regarded the process as a single one. Unlike John Bowlby, he did not need to be instructed "to make all one's points ... not only with pictures and examples and concrete nouns but literally with words of one syllable."[5]

His actual voice was high-pitched and slow (although most broadcast speech of the period sounds painfully slow to modern ears) and did not reflect his vitality. According to BBC audience research, many listeners judged it unpleasant, or even "awful".[6] He himself was deeply critical of the way he sounded. He wrote to Benzie in 1960, "I've just listened to Jealousy, and while I liked the script I HATED the voice."[7] It wasn't until a studio manager moved the microphone closer to Winnicott in 1960 that he declared "For the first time I did not hate hearing myself."[8]

Various explanations for Winnicott's voice have been advanced. Benzie speculated that one reason was his "lifelong professional habit of talking to mentally sick small children in a very very quiet way."[9] A producer who worked with him remembered that "He told me that ... when he was talking to the children they related to someone with a high voice better—someone like their mother, or a woman anyway."[10]

Yet Winnicott's voice also helped him communicate with mothers so that he did not sound like a declamatory male expert: it positioned him instead midway in pitch between a man and a woman. This vocal "no man's land" made him, in a sense, androgynous, combining the authority of a male doctor with a more supposedly "female" empathy.

It's curious that his talks engendered so little resistance when other psychoanalytically orientated broadcasts of the time almost invariably trailed controversies behind them. This is partly because he was championed by Benzie and Quigley, but also because he fitted the cultural renaissance represented by Penguin Books, the documentary film movement, and Mass Observation social research, as well as the BBC.

There were a number of other factors sheltering Winnicott from criticism. Until 1959 all his talks were transmitted on the Light Programme or the Home Service, and so were much less likely to be reviewed in the press than Third Programme broadcasts, especially if nestling under the rubric of daytime magazine programmes such as "Woman's Hour". His talks were also less likely to incite hostility because he did not advocate a rigid or novel child-rearing regime.

Winnicott broadcast anonymously, as was the custom of the time (Karpf, 1988), and was usually described as "speaking anonymously, as a psychologist",[11] although at other times as "a doctor caring for children",[12] and only infrequently as "a psychotherapist",[13] even though he was president of the British Psychoanalytical Society from 1956 until 1959. The camouflage of medicine and psychology suited him: it prevented listeners from being scared of what he had to say, or placing him within a particular analytic tradition, emphasising instead his medical expertise and his focus on normality.

Another reason that Winnicott found such a secure berth in the BBC was because psychoanalytic ideas had already begun to percolate into British society, with terms like Oedipus complex and ego common among intellectuals. The collective trauma of the First World War, as well as attempts to treat shell shock, had made the British public receptive to anything that might help explain the "fragility of reason" (Richards, 2000). Psychoanalytic ideas were also disseminated by the Bloomsbury set (Rodman, 2003): Lytton Strachey's younger brother, James Strachey, was Winnicott's analyst.

The spread of the child guidance movement in the 1920s and '30s, with its developmental view of childhood, had laid the foundations for Winnicott, while the arrival in Britain of Melanie Klein in 1926 and Freud in 1938 brought psychoanalysis more public recognition. By 1939, as W. H. Auden remarked, Freud was "no more a person now but a whole climate of opinion" (1966). Campaigns by interwar criminologists for penal reform, saturated with psychoanalytic thinking, also proved influential, helping to shape popular conceptions about how to treat delinquency (Waters, 1998)—an approach famously satirised by the 1957 Broadway musical *West Side Story* in Stephen Sondheim's lyrics for "Gee Officer Krupke": "This boy don't need a judge, he needs an analyst's care."

Zaretsky (1999) has called Winnicott "the first English analytic media celebrity". Certainly, as part of the British school of object relations theorists, his broadcasts offered a psychoanalysis that wasn't introspective (Thomson, 2006), or full of the dark Jewish mittel-European drives of Freud and Klein's destructive infant. He understood Englishness: "The Englishman", he wrote, "… does not want to be upset, to be reminded that there are personal tragedies all over the place, that he is not really happy himself, in short—he refuses to be put off his golf" (Phillips, 1988, p. 48).

If Winnicott was populariser-in-chief of psychoanalytic ideas about parenting, his was not a lone voice. Susan Isaacs and Ruth Thomas also took to the airwaves while *The Common Sense Book of Baby and Child Care*, the 1946 bestselling childcare manual by Benjamin Spock—an admirer of Winnicott—found a public eager to read about liberal child-rearing practices, and magazines such as *Childhood, the Magazine for Modern Parents* launched in 1947, followed.

But probably the most significant factor in creating a public receptive to Winnicott's broadcasts was the Second World War. Gone were the old certainties and traditional beliefs. Family life became a site of absence as well as presence: with men recruited and children evacuated, a public space was created in which the family could be thought about, and thought about differently. Women's role as keeper of the home and hearth became symbolically more important and more visible. People wanted to understand the origin of individual destructive instincts at a time when the consequences of collective aggression were so terrible. Perhaps Winnicott's wartime broadcasts, through their analysis of babies' feelings, acted also as a medium through which to express adults' confusion and fear, something otherwise hard to speak about in wartime when it was felt that public morale needed to be kept high: discussion of infants' angry and anxious states could therefore serve as a conduit through which their parents' similar emotions might be safely articulated and contained. Indeed, the same medium, as Farley has noted (2012), that blared out Hitler's hate-filled speeches and news of the progress of the war became the channel through which Winnicott could explore human vulnerability and sadness.

In 1940, as psychiatric consultant to the government evacuation scheme in Oxford, he supervised hostel workers' care of children separated from their mothers. For both Winnicott and the public, the removal of children from their homes and mothers threw into sharp relief what constituted good mothering—and what the reliable, continuing presence of a mother contributed to a child's emotional growth.

Among the many later criticisms of Winnicott is that he sounded patronising, as if he were talking to children and not just about them. It was rather the case, though, that he became one—his identification with the infant was uninhibitedly visceral.

Most mothers are probably neither as ordinary nor as devoted as Winnicott depicted them, but he must be read and listened to historically. His conception of "the ordinary devoted mother" is implicitly contrasted not with an "ordinary un-devoted mother" (Winnicott was rarely normative or judgemental about mothers in his broadcasts) but with an "extraordinary devoted mother": he was attempting to make visible, name, and hymn the routine practices of mothering, which he felt had been neglected and demanded wonder and respect. Yet he was also sensitive to the frustrations and even hatred that could be generated by caring for a baby—the sense of "Damn you, you little bugger" (2002, p. 7). And he could be radical in his attitudes to women: his view that a fear of women often followed from the refusal to acknowledge our early dependence on mothers was a startling idea for a male doctor in the 1950s (Winnicott, 1957).

Winnicott stopped broadcasting regularly in the early 1960s, partly because of ill health, but also because his ideas were also increasingly out of sync with changing social currents. Post-Spock, liberal parenting itself came to be problematised, with women beginning to critique the notion of maternal sacrifice (Thomson, 2012).

But by then the BBC and Winnicott had taken psychoanalysis out of the consulting room and onto the airwaves (Shapira, 2012). Anna Freud herself enthusiastically endorsed the broadcasts. "I admire your 'Devoted Mother' talks very much, and I feel no student of our subject should miss either reading or hearing them (Rodman, 2003, p. 271).

Winnicott, the quintessential Englishman among Europeans, with a talent for metabolising psychoanalytic ideas for lay listeners, had found a post-war female public for whom the home and mothering had become emblems of "normality". Winnicott was their guide through this new normal, and its eloquent rhapsodist.

Acknowledgements

I am grateful to the Winnicott Trust for a grant to research Donald Winnicott's radio broadcasts, and Lesley Caldwell, co-editor of *Winnicott's Collected Works* (OUP), in particular for her consistent encouragement. Thanks also to the BBC Written Archive at Caversham, for permission to quote from BBC copyright material, and to Louise North, indefatigable researcher in the Archive, for responding to my endless questions. Extracts from Dr Winnicott's letters are reproduced by permission of The Marsh Agency Ltd on behalf of the Winnicott Trust. Thanks too to the Donald Winnicott Collection, Oskar Diethelm Library, DeWitt Wallace Institute for the History of Psychiatry, Weill Cornell Medical College, New York, and its curator Marisa Sharai, for permission to quote from their papers, and to the Winnicott Trust for permission to access the Winnicott papers in the Wellcome Library, London. I am grateful to Angela Saward, curator of moving images and sound at the Wellcome Library, for copies of Winnicott's surviving broadcasts, and to Craig Fees of the Planned Environment Therapy Trust Archive for copies of the re-recordings of some of the broadcasts that Winnicott made for a New Zealand parents' organisation. I am also grateful to Helen Taylor-Robinson, co-editor of *Winnicott's Collected Works* for her help in answering questions.

Notes

1. BBC Donald Woods Winnicott Dr RCONT 1 File Ia 1943–1959 (hereafter TWa): Isa Benzie (IB) to Donald Winnicott (DW), 18.4.46.
2. Ibid. DW to Janet Quigley (JQ), 15.1.45.
3. BBC Microfiche, script (as broadcast) of "The Ordinary Devoted Mother and Her Baby—My Fan Mail", 20.2.52.
4. BBC RCONT1: TALKS—WINNICOTT, DONALD WOODS, DR. File 1b, 1960–1962 (hereafter TWb): quoted in IB to DW, 13.4.60.
5. BBC RCONT 1 John Bowlby Talks 1946–1962, File 1, IB to John Bowlby (JB), 15.4.46.
6. BBC Audience Research, "Parents and Children", op. cit.
7. TWb: DW to IB, 7.3.60.
8. TWb: DW to IB, 26.4.60.
9. TWb: IB to JQ, 3.5.60.
10. Personal communication, Sally Thompson, 13.1.13.
11. "Happy Children", *Radio Times*, 10.12.43, 4.2.44.
12. "How's The Baby?", *Radio Times*, 30.9.49; "The Ordinary Devoted Mother and Her Baby", *Radio Times*, 9.1.52.
13. "Difficult Children in Difficult Times", *Radio Times*, 26.1.45.

References

Auden, W. H. (1966). In Memory of Sigmund Freud. *Collected Shorter Poems 1927–1957*. London: Faber and Faber.
Farley, L. (2012). Analysis on air: A sound history of Winnicott in wartime. *American Imago*, 69(4): 449–471.
Karpf, A. (1988). *Doctoring the Media: the Reporting of Health and Medicine*. London: Routledge.
Matheson, H. (1933). *Broadcasting*. London: Thornton Butterworth.
Phillips, A. (1988). *Winnicott*. London: Fontana.
Richards, G. (2000). Britain on the couch: The popularization of psychoanalysis in Britain 1918–1940. *Science in Context*, 13(2): 183–230.
Rodman, F. R. (2003). *Winnicott: Life and Work*. Boston, MA: Da Capo Press.
Schwartz, J. (1999). *Cassandra's Daughter*. London: Penguin.
Sconce, J. (2009). Wireless ego: The pulp physics of psychoanalysis. In: D. R. Cohen & M. Coyle (Eds.), *Broadcasting Modernism* (pp. 31–50). Gainsville, FL: University Press of Florida.
Shapira, M. (2012). Psychoanalysts on the radio: domestic citizenship and motherhood in postwar Britain. In: J. Regulska & B. G. Smith (Eds.), *Women and Gender in Postwar Europe*. London: Routledge.
Spock, B. (2002). Introduction. In: D. W. Winnicott, *Winnicott on the Child*. Cambridge, MA: Perseus.
Thomson, M. (2006). *Psychological Subjects: Identity, Culture and Health in Twentieth Century Britain*. Oxford: Oxford University Press.
Thomson, M. (2012). Bowlbyism and the Postwar Settlement. Paper given at the Institute of Historical Affairs, London University.
Waters, C. (1998). Havelock Ellis, Sigmund Freud and the state: discourses of homosexual identity in interwar Britain. In: L. Bland & L. Doan (Eds.), *Sexology in Culture* (pp. 165–179). Cambridge: Polity Press.
Winnicott, C., Bollas, C., Davis, M., & Shepherd, R. (Eds.) (1993). Editors' preface. In: D. W. Winnicott, *Talking to Parents*. Cambridge, MA: Perseus.
Winnicott, D. W. (1957). The Child and the Family: First Relationships. In: D. W. Winnicott (2002), *The Mother's Contribution to Society*. Cambridge, MA: Perseus.
Winnicott, D. W. (1964). *The Child, the Family and the Outside World*. London: Pelican.
Winnicott, D. W. (1986). *Home Is Where We Start From*. London: Pelican.
Winnicott, D. W. (1993). *Talking to Parents*. Cambridge, MA: Perseus.
Winnicott, D. W. (2002). *Winnicott on the Child*. Cambridge, MA: Perseus.
Zaretsky, E. (1999). "One large secure, solid background": Melanie Klein and the origins of the British welfare state. *Psychoanalysis and History*, 1(2): 136–154.

CHAPTER ELEVEN

Winnicott's paradigm shift in psychoanalytic theory and practice

Zeljko Loparic

Winnicott's plea for a revolution in psychoanalysis

Shortly before his death, Winnicott pleaded for a revolution in psychoanalysis: "I am asking for a kind of revolution in our work. Let us re-examine what we do" (Abram, 2013, pp. 313–314). His reasons for making such a proposal were clinical: "It may be that in dealing with the repressed unconscious we are colluding with the patient and the established defences." We have to come to the conclusion, he adds, "that the common failure of many excellent analyses has to do with the patient's dissociation hidden in material that is clearly related to repression taking place as a defence in a seemingly whole person" (Abram, 2013, pp. 313–314).

Winnicott attributes the inefficiency of psychoanalytic problem-solving activity to the lack of a clear distinction between the repressed unconscious and another kind of unconscious: the dissociation of personality. Psychoanalysis has been in a crisis, due to insufficient diagnosis and inadequate treatment procedures. In order to recover, psychoanalytic theoretical framework for problem-solving should be changed in a revolutionary manner and so should psychoanalytic treatment procedures.

This raises the question as to which kind of revolutionary move must be undertaken. The one Winnicott had already produced. The shift was clearly recognised in 1968: "At the time of these BBC broadcasts in the late Forties, I was in a unique position, being able to see my patients in terms of both paediatrics and of a kind of psycho-analysis that was peculiarly my own" (Winnicott, 1993, p. xiv). From the late 1940s onwards, Winnicott's job was definitely to be himself, not a Kleinian or even a Freudian:

> I believe my views began to separate out from hers [M. Klein's], and in any case I found she had not included me in as a Kleinian. This did not matter to me because I have never been able to follow anyone else, not even Freud. (1965a, pp. 176–177)

Winnicott was a libertarian, not only in science but also in life, morals, religion, cultural matters, and with regard to tradition in general: "Mature adults bring vitality to that which is ancient, old, and orthodox by re-creating it after destroying it" (1965b, p. 94).

Winnicott called himself "a paediatrician who has swung to psychiatry, and a psychiatrist who has clung to paediatrics" (1958, p. 157), using "psychoanalysis as a ground-basis" (1984, p. 209). Psychoanalysis modified by Winnicott should be the guide for clinical practice in both of these disciplines, as well as in other areas, such as social work and public health policies and legislation. In addition, Winnicott made proposals regarding interdisciplinary training programmes and institutions capable of delivering this kind of training.

Psychoanalysis was practised by Winnicott as a science:

> I want to put before you the view that psychology simply means the study of human nature, and that it is a science, just as physics, physiology, and biology are sciences. This is my view, and my life's work is based on this assumption, for I think you ought to know at the outset that I am not only a doctor but also a psychoanalyst. (1996, p. 3)

But what does scientific work consist of?

> For the scientist every gap in understanding provides an exciting challenge. Ignorance is held, and a research programme is devised.

> The stimulus for the work done is the existence of the gap. The scientist can afford to wait and to be ignorant. For the scientist the formulation of questions is almost the whole thing. The answers, when found, only lead on to other questions. The nightmare of the scientist is the idea of complete knowledge. He shudders to think of such a thing. (1986, p. 14)

Psychoanalysis belongs to a group of scientific disciplines or practices such as education, paediatrics, psychiatry, psychology, psychotherapy, and social work, which use the same basic scientific strategy and for that reason differ from "religion, philosophy, poetry and alchemy [...]" (1996, p. 237).

Kuhn's framework for the scientific and philosophical study of Winnicott's Q&A game

In discussing Winnicott's proposal for a revolution in psychoanalysis as a scientific discipline, I and other authors (Bowlby, Greenberg, Mitchell, McDougall, Dias, Minhot, Abram, Eshel, among them) have found it useful to take into account the theory of scientific revolutions proposed by Kuhn. For Kuhn, science is a problem-solving activity within a scientific community guided by a research programme which has two main components: shared examples of successfully solved problems and constellations of group commitments, also called a "disciplinary matrix", consisting of guiding generalisations, operational ontologies, methodologies, and shared values. If there is a critical increase in unsolved problems in the "normal research", revolutionary research is initiated in order to formulate a new research programme. The acceptance of the new paradigm by the community, initially only by younger and peripheral members, is not a change of mind based on compelling theoretical arguments, but a conversion similar to a gestalt switch. The new paradigm is taught in the first place by means of shared exemplars.

Freud's and Winnicott's paradigms compared

Freud's exemplars are solved problems relating to the Oedipus complex, the shibboleth of psychoanalysis. In this way, the Freudian analyst wants to know about the patient's desires and wishes of a sexual nature in triangular relationships between whole persons, the representations of which have been made unconscious by repression. These "child in the mother's bed" problems, as I call them, are illustrated in Freud's case studies.

Winnicott's exemplars are solutions to the "problem of existing" related to maturational needs (being in contact, going on being in relationship, integrating, etc.), which have not initially been met in the baby's dual relationship with the environment-mother ("baby on the mother's lap" problems). More complex problems arise in successively broader environments, such as the Freudian triangular family situations, consisting of hold-ups of the maturational process due to environmental failures. Winnicott's case studies of these disorders are meant to be used as illustrations and teaching material (1971, p. 9).

Freud's guiding generalisation is, of course, his theory of sexuality, which includes the theory of the development of libido organisation and corresponding sexual objects.

Winnicott's guiding generalisation is his theory of maturational processes (integration into a personal whole together with physical growth and emotional and mental development) through which human nature exemplifies itself in time as a concrete human being able to become a spontaneous and creative individual, to have a life (including a sexual life) worth living and, eventually, to "afford to sacrifice spontaneity, even to die" (1958, p. 304).

Freud's initial and indeed paradigmatic ontological model of the human being consists of the psychical apparatus functioning as a reflex arc. In Freud's writings, deterministic reflex processes remain the model of psychical (i.e., mental) processes in general, spelled out in his metapsychology. The general schematic picture of the psychical apparatus is represented by Freud in the following way:

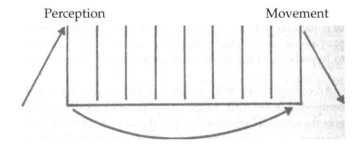

Winnicott's ontological model for thinking about and dealing with human beings is provided by his theory of human nature, which manifests itself in time through maturational processes. Some main universal features of human nature are essential aloneness, primary creativity, playing, potential space, psycho-somatic existence, tendency towards integration, tendency towards regression/and the circular structure of human life. The general structure of all maturational processes is already present in the mother's lap, as is depicted in the following drawing by Winnicott:

Differences between Freud's box model and Winnicott's lap model are clear. For Winnicott, a human being does not behave like a deterministic reflex apparatus. In human life, mind, mental structures, and mental functions are not fundamental. Winnicott's ontology of psychosomatic existence is experiential. It is formulated in his own descriptive language, not in "the terms of psycho-analytic metapsychology" (1987, p. 58).

Freud's clinical method is the *talking cure*, which consists of bringing the codified repressed unconscious stored in a dark compartment within the psychic apparatus to its conscious part, by means of free association on the part of the patient and interpretation (decoding the repressed unconscious) by the analyst. The setting is characterised mainly by the rule of abstinence. The whole procedure is conceived for the treatment of neuroses.

Winnicott's clinical methodology is the *care-cure*. It aims at facilitating the patient's integration process to restart at the point where it broke down, by 1) unfreezing of rigid defences and defence organisations, 2) giving the patient the needed provision, 3) helping the patient to feel real, to modify or even establish the relationship with the external world for the first time, to be able to end the analysis and to take care of him- or herself, 4) preventing of the breakdown at any stage. The solution is brought about by the "behaviour" of the analyst and/or of the actual environmental, providing the care which was required by the patient at a certain point of time in the past, but which was not offered. To this effect, the setting, "the summation of all details of management", individual or environmental (1958, p. 297), is more important than the interpretation.

Freud's values may be divided into clinical (freeing the patient of symptoms and suffering), general (realisation of the pleasure principle programme, that is, of the aim of life) and "higher" values (cultural values achieved by sublimation).

Winnicott's values include personal integration, taking care of other people, social integration, caring for the cultural heritage, self-realisation, and eventually "growing downwards" and being able even to die. In essence, there is only one value: the life worth living.

Compared to Freudian psychoanalysis, Winnicott's psychoanalysis presents the following distinctive features: new concept of psychic disorders, a new guiding generalisation, new ontology, new treatment procedures, new values, new training programme, new applications.

Is Winnicott's paradigm still psychoanalysis? Yes, because it is about the unconscious and also about recollecting and history taking. No, if the "unconscious" according-to-Winnicott (dissociation of personality due to the interruption of the maturational process) is not accepted because it is irreconcilable with the Freudian unconscious; and also if recollecting and history taking is not allowed to encompass collecting oneself and history making. Unity of the psychotherapeutic field is a value, but not at any price:

> I am concerned with everything that makes *against* cohesion. I would like to make it seem to be a miracle that the group claims to be a group. If there is mutual suspicion, then I want to examine mutual suspicion. The risk has to be taken that, if we look at ourselves, we actually disintegrate. But if we fail to take this risk, then we are bound together by a fear of disunity, which is a negation factor. (1996, pp. 237–238)

Freud's and Winnicott's applied psychoanalyses

The main thesis of Freud's applied psychoanalysis states that the beginnings of religion, morals, society, and art are found in the Oedipus complex, in full agreement with his claim that this complex constitutes the core of all neuroses (*Totem and Taboo*, 1912–13, part IV).

The main thesis of Winnicott's applied psychoanalysis is that social order and culture result from the maturational processes facilitated by environmental provision and enriched by tradition, which is used both destructively and creatively. In particular, Winnicott maintains that monotheism has its roots in pre-oedipal stages:

> [...] I suggest that the baby is likely to make use of the father as a blueprint for his or her own integration when just becoming at times a unit. [...] In this way one can see that the father can be the first glimpse for the child of integration and of personal wholeness. It is easy to go from this interplay between introjections and projection to the important concept in the world's history of a one god, monotheism, not a one god for me and another one god for you. (1989, p. 243)

With regard to morals, Winnicott defends the thesis of "innate morality", according to which "[W]e do need to abandon absolutely the theory that children can be born innately amoral" (1984, p. 111). When healthy, "… the child develops in a very complicated way a sense of right and wrong and a capacity for experiencing a sense of guilt; and each child has ideals, and has an idea of what he or she wants for the future" (1984, p. 149). The sense of right and wrong, related to the sense of responsibility, forms the basis of the ethics of care, which is the original meaning of ethics, the Kantian and the Freudian ethics of law (justice) being secondary and derived.

Winnicottian communities and institutions

In 1968, Balint envisioned the creation of a "managing school" of analysts who think of clinical disorders as "due to mismanagement of the child during his early formative period by the adults, above all by his mother" (p. 110). He added:

> True, the "managing" school can hardly be called a school because, in contrast to the two previous ones, it lacks any organization or cohesion and, in consequence, has not developed a proper language of its own, although there are signs that this may happen under the influence of Winnicott's ideas. (p. 116)

In 1968, these words by Balint might have sounded as an exhortation, today they look more like a prophecy. Indeed, several Winnicottian institutions exist: the Squiggle Foundation (1981), the Winnicott Trust (1984), the Brazilian Society for Winnicottian Psychoanalysis (2005), International Winnicott Association (2013, eighteen member groups), Brazilian, French, Chinese, and Israeli training courses, the Brazilian Annual Winnicott Colloquia (since 1995), and IWA International Winnicott Congresses (started 2015).

References

Abram, J. (2013). *Donald Winnicott Today*. London: Routledge.
Balint, M. (1968). *The Basic Fault*. Evanston, IL.: Northwestern University Press, 1992.
Freud, S. (1912–13). *Totem and Taboo. S. E., 13*. London: Hogarth.
Winnicott, D. W. (1958). *Through Paediatrics to Psychoanalysis: Collected Papers*. London: Karnac, 1975.
Winnicott, D. W. (1965a). *The Maturational Processes and the Facilitating Environment: Studies in the Theory of Emotional Development*. London: Karnac, 1990.
Winnicott, D. W. (1965b). *The Family and Individual Development*. London: Tavistock.
Winnicott, D. W. (1971). *Therapeutic Consultations in Child Psychiatry*. London: Hogarth.
Winnicott, D. W. (1984). *Deprivation and Delinquency*. London: Tavistock-Routledge.
Winnicott, D. W. (1986). *Home Is Where We Start From*. London: Penguin.
Winnicott, D. W. (1987). *The Spontaneous Gesture: Selected Letters of D. W. Winnicott*. Cambridge, MA: Harvard University Press.
Winnicott, D. W. (1989). *Psycho-Analytic Explorations*. London: Karnac, 2010.
Winnicott, D. W. (1993). *Talking to Parents*. Reading, MA: Addison-Wesley.
Winnicott, D. W. (1996). *Thinking about Children*. London: Karnac.

INDEX

Abram, J., 133
aesthetic form, 70–71 *see also* form in artistic creation, role of
aesthetic truth, 65–69
"agent, the", 14
aggression, 33
   in children, 53–56
   and initiation of relationship with external reality, 36
Ainsworth, M., 56
Alvarez, A., 98
art
   object, 70
   and psychoanalysis, 74
   and self-attunement, 71–73
   and self-discovery, 69–70
Arteche, A., 57, 58
attachment theory, 56
attuning forms, 73 *see also* form in artistic creation, role of
Auden, W. H., 127
authentic creation, 67 *see also* form in artistic creation, role of

auto-eroticism, 6
Ayling, S., 116

Baatz, S., 112
baby, 50 *see also* child development
   and relationships support
   brain responses to, 50
   and parents interactions, 55
   signs of ability to be in relationship with people, 51
   talk, 50
Baker, F., 116
Balint, M., 92, 140
Baranes, J. J., 18
Basho, M., 68, 71, 84
Baxter, S., 112
"being a subject", 18
Bell, C., 71
Benzie, I. D., 113–114
Blake, W., 85
Bollas, C., 10, 19, 126
Bolognini, S., 18, 19, 22, 27
Bonaminio, V., 31, 42

book-sharing, 58–60
Botella, C., 97, 98, 99
Botella, S., 97, 98
Bowlby, J., 56, 126, 130, 135
Brailsford, M. R., 116
brain responses to babies, 50
Britton, K., 87
Busch, F., 24

"capacity to be alone", 39
care-cure, 138
care of "sufficiently good mother", 3
child development and relationships support, 49
    aggression in children, 53–56
    attachment theory, 56
    babies and parents interactions, 55
    baby talk, 50
    book-sharing, 58
    brain responses to babies, 50
    capacity for concern, 55
    clinical implications, 58–60
    cognitive development, 57–58
    development of secure attachment, 56–57
    domains of child development, 52
    emotion regulation and self-control, 53–56
    mismatch-repair process, 54
    parental physical holding, 54
    parenting on, 49
    reflective functioning, 57
    scaffolding, 58
    sensitive parenting, 51
    signs of baby in relationship with people, 51
    social understanding, 52–53
    theory of mind, 52
Chodorkoff, B., 112
Clancier, L., xx
cognitive development, 57–58
Coleridge, S. T., 81
concept of regression, 91, 103
    analyst's presence, 96
    case of Bob, 100–103
    clinical vignette, 94–103

dead mother complex, 97–98
    psyche and soma, 93–94
    regredience, 98–100, 103
    theory of the dream process, 93
    therapeutic regression, 92
    topographical regression, 91, 93
concern, the capacity for, 55
confused perceptual identity, 78
Constructions in Analysis, 3
Cooper, P. J., 57, 58, 59, 60
countertransference, 32, 36 *see also* transference
creative activity
    apperception varieties, 84
    metapsychological analysis of process of, 9–10
creativity
    and abstracting forms, 75
    destruction in service of, 81–82
    dialectic creativity/destructivity, 12–14
    formlessness and, 10–12
    hallucination relation with sexual and, 5
    inherited potential for, 79–80
    object survival and dialectic, 12–14
    and transitional phenomena, 64
creativity/destructivity, dialectic, 12–14
creativity in everyday life, 77, 87–88
    confused perceptual identity, 78
    destruction in service of creativity, 81–82
    discovering ourselves and world in ourselves, 82–83
    experiencing with bodily self, 83–84
    inherited potential for creativity, 79–80
    inherited tendencies, 81
    between inner and external world, 87
    "Red Wheelbarrow, The", 80–81
    sense of reality as frame, 84–86
    spontaneous living example, 80–81
    transference as playground, 86–87
    transitional object, 80

transitional phenomena, 77–79, 80
varieties of creative apperception, 84
Winnicott's paradox, 77
Croudace, T., 58

Dadomo, H., 60
Davis, M., 126
dead mother complex, 97–98
delirium, 3, 4
De Pascalis, L., 60
dialectical dynamisms, 38
Di Renzo, M., 42
disciplinary matrix, 135
discovering ourselves in world and world in ourselves, 82–83
dissociation, 4
  in personality, 41
dreams, 3

"Ego Distortion in Terms of True and False Self", 33
Eliot, T. S., 83
emergence of love proper, 14
emotion and self-control, 53–56
empty void, 27
Enriquez, M., 18
envy and envious attacks, 5
experience of "survival", 2
experiencing with bodily self, 83–84

Fabozzi, P., 31, 33, 36
Faimberg, H., 18
false reparation, 41
Farley, L., 128
Fearon, P., 57, 58
Ferenczi, S., 92
first *not-me* possession, 37
Flam, J., 75
Fonda, P., 22
form in artistic creation, role of, 63
  aesthetic form, 70–71
  aesthetic truth, 65–69
  art and psychoanalysis, 74
  art and self-attunement, 71–73
  art and self-discovery, 69–70
  art object, 70
  attuning forms, 73
  authentic creation, 67
  creativity and abstracting forms, 75
  infant's "vitality affects", 73
  Matisse, H., 66
  perfect form, 66
  "presentational symbols" by moment experience, 73
  primary creativity and transitional phenomena, 64
  transference phenomena, 64
"formless" space, 11
formlessness and creativity, 10–12
Foster, C., 84
"found/created" process, 4, 5
  variant of, 8
Freud, A., 40, 80
Freud, S., 1, 83, 85, 92, 111
  applied psychoanalysis, 139
  auto-eroticism, 6
  box model vs. Winnicott's lap model, 138
  exemplars, 135
  first urgency of psyche, 11
  Freudian vs. Winnicott's psychoanalysis, 138–139
  Freud's box model vs. Winnicott's lap model, 138
  hallucinatory process, 6
  illusion, 6
  paradigmatic ontological model, 136
  perception and hallucination, 3
  "psychic work", 12
  psychoanalysis and psychoanalytic theory vs. suggestions, 3
  psychology and, 3
  talking cure, 138
  values, 138
  and Winnicott's applied psychoanalyses, 139–140
  and Winnicott's paradigms compared, 135–139
  vs. Winnicott's psychoanalysis, 138–139

function of the mother's face, 8
fundamental Winnicottian concepts, 35

Giannakoulas, A., 38
Gilbert, M., 111
Gillespie, W. H., xix
Goodyer, I., 57
Green, A., 19, 97
Greenberg, J., 21
Greenson, R. R., 27
Guss Teicholz, J., 19, 22

Halligan, S., 57, 58
hallucination, 3, 4, 6
  relation with sexuality and
    creativity, 5
  "sumbulon", 7
  wish-fulfilment, 5
"Hate in the Countertransference",
  31–33, 35–36, 42
hate towards patient, 31–42
  aggression, 33
  countertransference, 32
  dialectical dynamisms, 38
  false reparation, 41
  first not-me possession, 37
  "Hate in Countertransference",
    31–33, 35–36, 42
  identification and analysis in
    emotional development, 34
  "limits" of potential space, 38
  manic defence, 40
  mother's psychic functioning for
    baby's development, 34
  personality dissociation, 41
  psychopathological dispositions,
    39
  relationship initiation with external
    reality, 36
  "subjective object", 37
  transference–countertransference
    relationship, 35
  transitional object, 36–38
  Winnicottian concepts, 35
Heaney, S., 69
Hernandez, M., 38
Hodgkin, H., 85

holding, parental physical, 54
Hooper, R., 58
Hudson, A., 116

Ich see subject
id, 2
identification and analysis of
  processes in emotional
  development, 34
illusion, 6
impersonal pronoun, use of, 26
infant's "vitality affects", 73
inherited tendencies, 81
inner and external world dialogue, 87
internal and external reality bridging, 4
interpsychic dialogue, 17
  anecdote, 19–20
  "being a subject", 18
  interpsychic, intersubjective,
    interpersonal, 18–19
  interpsychic, the, 19
  interpsychic dimension, 22
  interpsychic exchange, 18
  minimal technical tools, 23–28
  otherness, the, 20
  person, 18
  proposals, different functional/
    relational levels, 21–23
  reflections in clinic, 21
  subject, 18
  transpsychic relationship, 18
intersubjectivist, 21

Jones, E., 112, 113, 115

Kaës, R., 18
Kahr, B., 112, 116
Kalmanovitch, J., xx
Karpf, A., 127
Kempton, C., 58
Klein, M., 5, 31
  "Notes on Some Schizoid
    Mechanisms", 31, 33
Kuhn, A., 63, 135
  framework for scientific and
    philosophical study of
    Winnicott's Q&A game, 135

Landman, M., 59
Langer, S., 70, 73, 74
Lanyado, M., 98
Leavis, F. R., 87
"limits" of space, 38
Losso, R., 18
love proper, emergence of, 14

MacCarthy, B., 112
MacLachlan, B., 60
MacLeish, A., 65
Maddox, B., 112
manic defence, 40
maternal care components, 7
maternal environment, adaptation of, 12, 13
maternal preoccupation, primary, 5
Matheson, H., 124
Matisse, H., 66
McPherson, K., 59
media psychology, 115
Merleau-Ponty, M., 73
Micati, L., 26
Millar, W. M., 112
Milner, M., 8, 84
mind, theory of, 52
minimal technical tools, 23 see also interpsychic dialogue
    "Mmmmh ...!" sound, 26–27
    phrases for clarification, 23–26
    repeating the patient, 27–28
    use of impersonal pronoun, 26
    use of "we", 28
mirroring, 8, 70–74
    parental, 52–53
"mirror-role of mother", 47
mismatch-repair process, 54
"Mmmmh ...!" sound, 26–27
Molteno, C., 59
Morrell, J., 56
mother's face, function of, 8
mother's psyche in baby's development, 34
Murray, L., 49, 56, 57, 58, 59, 60

Narrow Road to the Deep North, The, 68
Neve, M., 116

"Notes on Some Schizoid Mechanisms", 31, 33
not-me, 37, 38, 48

object survival and dialectic creativity/destructivity, 12–14
otherness, the, 20

parenting
    on child development, 49
    physical holding, 54
    sensitive, 51
perception, 3, 4
    and hallucination, 3, 4
perceptual identity, 78
perfect form, 66 see also form in artistic creation, role of
person, 18
personality dissociation, 41
Phillips, A., 124, 128
phrases for clarification, 23–26
pliable medium, 8, 10, 11
Polanyi, M., 87
"presentational symbols" by moment experience, 73
primary creativity and transitional phenomena, 64
primary maternal preoccupation, 5
psyche, first urgency of, 11
"psychic work", 12
psychoanalysis, 133, 134 see also shift in psychoanalytic theory and practice
    applied, 139
    Freudian vs. Winnicott's, 138–139
    and general public, 111
    and psychoanalytic theory vs. suggestions, 3
    revolution in, 133–135
    as science, 134
psychoanalysts and media, 112
Pudney, J., 116
pure feminine, 10

Rapp, D., 112
reality as frame, sense of, 84–86
"Red Wheelbarrow, The", 80–81

reflective functioning, 57
regrediance, 98–100, 103
repeating the patient, 27–28
Richards, G., 127
Rickman, J., 112
Ries, P., 112
Rodman, F., 37
Rodman, F. R., 125, 127
Rycroft, C., 93

sameness and otherness, between
 see interpsychic dialogue
scaffolding, 58
Schlögler, B., 82
Schopenhauer, A., 78
Schwartz, J., 125
science, 135
 psychoanalysis practiced as a, 134
Sconce, J., 126
secure attachment development, 56–57
Segal, H., 19
Seldes, G., 112
self, 1–2 *see also* subject
 development of, 48, 88
 experiencing bodily, 83–84
 in mother's face, 74
 in poetry, 69
Self, experience of, 21–22
Self/Not-Self modulation, 17, 19–20, 27
sense of being, 2–5
Shakespeare, W., 84
Shapira, M., 129
Shepherd, R., 126
shift in psychoanalytic theory
 and practice, 133
 care-cure, 138
 Freudian vs. Winnicott's
  psychoanalysis, 138–139
 Freud's and Winnicott's applied
  psychoanalyses, 139–140
 Freud's and Winnicott's paradigms,
  135–139
 Freud's box model vs. Winnicott's
  lap model, 138
 Freud's values vs. Winnicott's
  values, 138

 Kuhn's framework for scientific
  and philosophical study of
  Winnicott's Q&A game, 135
 talking cure, 138
 Winnicott and Freud ontological
  model, 136–137
 Winnicottian communities and
  institutions, 140
 Winnicott's plea for revolution in
  psychoanalysis, 133–135
Simon, J. S., 116
singularity of primary relationship, 9
social understanding, 52–53
Spock, B., 125
spontaneous living, 80–81
Stein, A. L., 59
Stern, D., 10, 73, 74
subject, 1–2
 adaptation of maternal
  environment, 12, 13
 "agent, the", 14
 emergence and conception of, 1
 experience of "survival", 2
 formlessness and creativity, 10–12
 "formless" space, 11
 "found/created", 4, 5, 8
 function of mother's face, 8
 hallucination, 5–9
 metapsychological analysis of
  creative activity, 9–10
 perception and hallucination, 3, 4
 pliable medium, 8, 10, 11
 primary maternal preoccupation, 5
 sense of being, 2–5
 singularity of primary
  relationship, 9
 "subjective sensation", 6
 survival of object and dialectic
  creativity/destructivity, 12–14
subjective object, 37
subjective sensation, 6
survival, experience of, 2
survival of the object, 12–14
surviving, 13
Swartz, L., 59
Szasz, T., 64

talking cure, 138
theoretical-clinical thinking, 39
therapeutic regression, 92
Thomson, M., 128, 129
Tomlinson, M., 59, 60
topographical regression, 91, 93
transference, 34, 35 *see also* countertransference
—countertransference relationship, 35
phenomena, 64
as playground, 86–87
transitional object, 36–38, 80
transitional phenomena, 77–79, 80
transpsychic relationship, 18 *see also* interpsychic dialogue
Trevarthen, C., 82
Trevelyan, H., 113

universality of experience, 26

Vally, Z., 60
values, 138
Volkov, P., 116

Waters, C., 127
we, use of, 28
Widlöcher, D., 19
Williams, W. C., 80, 82
Willoughby, R., xx
Winnicott, C., 116, 126
Winnicott, D. W., 1, 134 *see also* shift in psychoanalytic theory and practice; Winnicott as broadcaster
aggression, 33
applied psychoanalysis, 139
as broadcaster, 111–117, 123–129
"capacity to be alone", 39
care-cure, 138
care of "sufficiently good mother", 3
components of maternal care, 7
countertransference, 32
dissociation in personality, 4, 41
"Ego Distortion in Terms of True and False Self", 33
emergence of love proper, 14
envy and envious attacks, 5
exemplars, 136
false reparation, 41
"found/created", 4, 5
Freudian vs. Winnicott's psychoanalysis, 138–139
and Freud ontological model, 136–137
fundamentals of Winnicott's theory, 123
fundamental Winnicottian concepts, 35
hallucinatory wish-fulfilment, 5
"Hate in the Countertransference", 31–33, 35–36, 42, 125
manic defence, 40
meeting with, 45–48
metapsychological analysis of creative activity, 9–10
mirroring, 71–72
"mirror-role of mother", 47
mother's face function, 8
mother's psychic functioning in baby's development, 34
ontological model of, 137
perception and hallucination, 4
primary maternal preoccupation, 5
"psychic work", 12
psychoanalysis as science, 134
"pure feminine", 10
revolutionary ideas, 31
theoretical-clinical thinking, 39
values, 138
Winnicottian leitmotifs, 34
Winnicott as broadcaster, 111
anonymous broadcast, 127
arresting phrases, 125
broadcasting career, 124
Devoted Mother talks, 129
family support, 113
"holding environment" for listeners, 124
inspirations, 116–117
letter to Miss Isa Benzie, 113–114

new cultural form of radio talk, 124–125
pioneering radio talks for BBC, 112
skill of writing to speak, 126
voice, 126
wartime broadcasts, 128
Winnicottian communities and institutions, 140
Winnicottian concepts, 35
Winnicottian institutions, 140
Winnicottian leitmotifs, 34

Winnicott's paradox, 77 *see also* creativity in everyday life
Winnicott, V., 113
Woodward, C., 60
Woolgar, M., 58, 59
Wright, K., 64

Yalom, I., 26
Yorke, J., 86
Young, M. L., 112

Zaretsky, E., 127